Weeds
in the
Wilderness

Weeds in the Wilderness

Growing Up in Rural Oklahoma

Tom Sherrill

1553 E. 19th, Tulsa, Oklahoma 74120

Copyright © 2014 by Tom Sherrill

All rights reserved, including the right of reproduction in whole
or in part in any form

Manufactured in the United States

Published in 2014 by Prairie Moon Press

Library of Congress Catalog Number: 2014941668

ISBN: 978-0-692-22655-1

Front Cover Photo (left to right): Tom Sherrill, Sharon Sherrill,
Laddy, and Gary Sherrill

*Dedicated to my wife, Pat Cahill Sherrill,
for bringing me out of the wilderness*

ACKNOWLEDGMENTS

Thanks go to my daughters Carrie Koewing Modrak and Shannon Sherrill Tolliver. Carrie did the initial edit of my book before rushing off to Africa to serve as a Peace Corps Volunteer and the final edit of the proof copy. Shannon was instrumental in locating pictures pertaining to our family history. To all the rest of my family and friends, thank you for listening to my stories all these years. A special thanks to Kathleen Price for taking my rough draft and turning it into a book.

TABLE OF CONTENTS

PREFACE

I was raised by caring parents. They provided me with everything a child could want. The only thing wrong was I rarely saw them. Let me explain. My mother was a talented, aggressive woman. My dad was equally as talented and hard working. They worked long hours, seven days a week. I could write a book on their accomplishments. But for now, this is my story.

When I was born, my family lived in Tulsa, Oklahoma. My dad, who was raised in Arkansas, always wanted to be "back on the farm." So one day in 1947, we moved out of a lovely debt-free home in a wonderful neighborhood to the WILDERNESS, a poor farming community next to a town of approximately two hundred people. A move of only thirty miles took us back in time one hundred years. We had no running water, no indoor plumbing, and the most amazing thing was a crank telephone. Our new phone number was two shorts and a long.

As I tell this strange story, try to understand that I love and care for my parents, and I understand why they were the way they were. Also remember that my parents, like thousands of others, were raised during the terrible depression in this country. When World War II began, lots of young women left their jobs as housewives and full-time mothers. They went to work in the bomber plants or took other war related jobs. After the war some of the women never went back to being housewives. This had a compelling effect on millions of war babies born during that era.

After the war America was never the same. We didn't realize it at the time, but our country would greatly change in the next twenty years. The change began with kids like me. I was five years old in 1947, just beginning a life filled with both humorous and tragic adventures and many wild and crazy times with unbelievable friends. I have always wondered how my life would have been different had I been raised in that lovely home in the city. Instead, I and my two older siblings, Gary and Sharon, were left to grow like weeds in the wilderness.

PART ONE

The Early Years

1

Down on the Farm

I can still remember my mother sitting on the back porch of our old run-down farmhouse crying like a baby. Dad had spent every cent they had to buy this large piece of property, but the years of harsh weather and the constantly blowing prairie wind had taken their toll on our farm. The grass and horse weeds were as tall as a grown man. The farmhouse and outbuildings had not been painted or repaired in years. Most of the fences and working pens were *beyond* repair.

My mother made up her mind that she would do what she had to do to make us look rich, even if it meant a major remodel. First she fixed the front of the house to look like a southern mansion from the road. Then she tore out the back of the house. That year we lived behind a billboard. We looked great from the road, but we were freezing out back. The project began in the middle of winter when we had run out of money and propane, so we used blankets and cardboard across the back of the house to keep out the cold.

Our only heat sources were a large fireplace and the propane heater. Inevitably we ran out of propane in the middle of the night when it was below zero. The propane had to be ordered and delivered by a truck.

Without the propane heater, we had to huddle up around the fireplace in order to stay warm. We spent many long hours around that fireplace. One night an old rancher stopped by while out looking for a stray cow. He joined us by the fire and told us stories about living in Oklahoma Indian Territory before statehood.

My dad never bought sticks of firewood. He went to Collinsville, another small town north of our farm, that had a sawmill where he could buy side cuts of logs twelve feet long. We used a crosscut saw to cut them down to size. Of course we always waited until it was freezing before doing this chore. I remember it being so cold several times that Dad just carried in some twelve foot pieces and put them in the fireplace. They stuck out in the living room and we just moved them in as they burned.

Besides being cold, the old farm house was scary. The wind frightened me. It never stopped blowing. My dad used to say that a barbed wire fence was the only thing between our farm and the North Pole—and it was down. The trees leaned south from years of fighting the cold north wind. Another thing that scared me was our front door that faced north. Its metal weather stripping made a high shrill noise when the wind blew like something out of a horror movie. Even scarier were the loose boards and branches that blew against the house. About the only other noise was an occasional cow bellowing in the dark like it was on its last leg.

Adding to my sense of isolation was the fact that my parents worked long hours in the real estate business. They never knew what time they could leave their office or what time they would be home. For a five-year-old boy all by himself for hours at night, the noises in our rickety house were almost too much. I tried many times to find a corner to sit in so nobody could sneak up on me, but this never worked. I was terrified until I finally found a great place to hide. We had a mulberry orchard in the back of our house. I turned on all the lights in the house and went out back and climbed one of the mulberry trees. I spent lots of nights waiting for my parents to get home, and then running in the house when they arrived and acting like I was okay. For years I had trouble buying shoes because my feet were shaped like those of a bird from all the hours of sitting in those trees.

As the remodel of our house progressed, I discovered a better place to hide until my parents came home at night. Years later I found out they had been terrified to come home one night and find me on top of an unfinished house thirty feet off the ground. That was about the time we got the new piano. Even when my parents didn't have enough money to heat the house, they always found the money when it was important to look good. One afternoon a big truck pulled into our farm and two men jumped out and began unloading a huge piano. Bringing it into the house was a snap; all they had to do was move the blankets and cardboard that defined the back of the house and set the piano in place.

My mother could sing and play the piano. She once had an audition with the great opera singer Lily Pons. Late that night when my mother arrived home, she was thrilled to see her new piano. She began playing and singing opera. It was like being at Carnegie Hall. Every time she would play and sing, I would sneak in and crawl under the piano and listen to every word. I loved it because it gave me a feeling of security. This same piano has followed me through life. To my amazement, a few months ago I crawled under it for old time's sake and it felt great.

Having left a typical suburban neighborhood in Tulsa, I missed having playmates who lived nearby. Our nearest neighbor lived about a mile away, so it was hard to meet kids my age. Naturally I was excited about my first day of school. I stayed awake most of the night thinking about riding on the school bus and maybe meeting some new friends. Mom really fixed us up. Gary, Sharon, and I looked like we were going to a fancy private school. I had on knickers (or knee pants) with socks up to my calves. My pants had no belt, but instead they had elastic waistbands built in. Gary and Sharon were dressed the same. We looked sharp.

We waited for the school bus on the side of the road in front of our house. Though it was called a road, it was dirt, no gravel, and had ruts two feet deep made by the milk trucks' early morning pickups from nearby dairies. Finally we saw it—a big, bright, Halloween orange bus making its way down our dusty path! It pulled up and stopped. With all the enthusiasm in the world, we jumped on the bus only to see nine or ten of the poorest looking kids we had ever seen dressed in overalls, some wearing no shoes. We stood at the front of the bus while they pointed and fell in the aisles laughing at us—the new oddly dressed kids who had just moved into the wilderness that we shared.

My first day of school was hell. Every time I let go of my pants someone else would pull them down. I must have been "depanted" a hundred times. On the bus ride home an older kid strangled me until I almost passed out. I knew if I was to survive in the wilderness, I would have to change my ways. We arrived home on the bus after school between five and six o'clock, depending on how drunk the bus driver was. He stopped and bought all the kids candy or gum if we promised not to tell on him. (He later became the town police chief.)

I have a vivid memory of a morning when another new kid was riding the school bus. We noticed something peculiar about the way he looked. After we'd been on the bus a while, he shocked us all by taking out his eye! Then he stuck the eye in his mouth and slowly pushed it back out. It looked like he had a real eye in his mouth. None of us had ever seen a fake eye, and we all wanted to look at it and touch it. We begged him to do something else funny with his eye and he didn't let us down. He got tickled and spit his eye out and it rolled down under the seats on the sticky, dirty bus floor. The bus driver stopped until the boy found his eye up front and then he just stuck it back in his eye socket.

In time I learned how to fit in better among our distant neighbors and I gradually grew to like our school. It was a three-story building constructed in 1908 out of wood. The floors creaked so loud when we walked on them, it sounded like they were on the brink of caving in. All the windows were wide open and had no screens. Sometimes the horse flies were so bad we couldn't hold class. Looking north out of the third story window, all a person could see was miles of wide open prairie. The big city skyline of Tulsa in the distance could barely be seen to the south, looking like two large ships on a sea of prairie.

Some days when the wind blew out of the east, we could hardly stay in our classroom due to the smell from the row of outhouses. Someone was using his head when he thought not to put the outhouses on the north or south side of school. The wind always blew out of the north in the winter, and in the summer it came from the south. I never got used to using an outhouse, either at home or at school. I put it off for as long as I could. For me, "being regular" meant going to the outhouse once a week.

Springtime marked the beginning of tornado season. The lightning on the prairie was awesome. One hot and humid afternoon, I went up on top of our house to check out the prairie. I could see for miles from this vantage point. In the distance I saw a bad storm moving in fast. Then the storm turned into a beautiful tornado. It was almost a gray, transparent color whipping back and forth. Then it hit the ground and changed to something black and ugly. Before I could get down from the top of the house, the tornado had hit our lake and sucked up the water, fish, and frogs and dumped them on me and our house. Lucky for us, the tornado lifted up before hitting the house. The next morning I learned the tornado had hit our school; it was now a two-story building. We had to finish the school year in a small church down the street. It was utter chaos having all classes in one room.

2

Siblings on our Own

Since my brother Gary was the eldest of the three of us, he must have thought he was supposed to take care of Sharon and me. We would have been better off if Adolf Hitler had been our baby-sitter. Gary had rules. If we disobeyed, we went to jail. Jail in our house was a closet that had no lights, very little air, and a door handle that only worked from the outside. Gary would lock Sharon and me in this closet many times for hours.

Sharon had a terrible time dealing with the closet. She couldn't get enough air, so she would put her face close to the small crack at the bottom of the door. Sometimes Gary would stuff rags in the crack to make Sharon scream and panic. One day Gary learned a new trick to play on us. He put us in jail and then went downstairs and began to play a Rachmaninoff song on the new piano. When the music started, Sharon realized Gary couldn't hear her screams over the piano and this drove her crazy. Just as our parents arrived in the driveway, Gary would run up the stairs and release us, crying and begging us not to tell on him. Like fools we felt sorry for him and never told. I think he learned this trick from our bus driver. Even today if Sharon or I hear a Rachmaninoff song, we get a feeling of claustrophobia.

When our parents wanted to have a few friends over, they offered to take Gary, Sharon, and me to the movies. Most kids would jump up and down with excitement, but instead, we hid. The movie was located in Collinsville about six miles away. When the last feature was over around ten o'clock, we went over to the B&H cafe and called our parents to come and get us. After a few hours and numerous calls, the cafe closed, so we went outside and sat on the curb to wait. The only other thing open at that time of night was the bar next door to the cafe. One night while waiting on the curb, we heard two drunks in the bar having an argument over how many times one of them had played the same record over and over again. We counted fourteen times before they threw the guy out. The song he liked so much was "The Tennessee Waltz." The drunk came over and sat on the curb alongside us. I guess he was waiting on a ride too.

Sitting on that curb, looking down the deserted main street waiting for a pair of headlights, I wondered why my parents didn't care, and why didn't my feet reach the pavement? All my waiting in fear of abandonment still compels me to be early wherever I go. I have to be careful not to upset people, but something inside me almost makes this a matter of life or death.

As we got a little older, we persuaded our parents to let us stay home on party nights, as long as we agreed to stay out of sight. This was much safer. We would go out to the car where we could listen to the radio, and finally we went upstairs to bed. The car wasn't bad because we liked the "Grand Ole Opry" and the "Louisiana Hay Ride," great live radio programs.

By midnight our parents' parties would usually get rocking and I would sneak halfway down the steps to watch through the balusters on the stairway. One night two old guys were arguing about who was born in the worst snow storm. One said, "I was born in the worst snow storm in the history of Oklahoma."

The other fellow, having had an equal amount to drink, yelled, "Do you want to see it snow?" He grabbed the first guy's coat, threw it on the floor, and peed all over it!

Often someone would accidently get locked in the bathroom and I would hear them yelling and screaming. I now suspect that our location in the middle of the wilderness was probably the reason our parents' parties got out of hand.

Sometime in the early fifties, Dad brought home a television set. This was one of the most exciting moments of my life. It was about the size of a refrigerator, but the picture tube was only six inches wide. At first we had only one channel and we never knew when the programs began. We spent many hours watching the test pattern. In the daytime it was impossible to see the picture, so we would throw an old blanket (usually a hot, sticky army blanket) over the television and get under it with the set. This worked great except that it was hot as hell during an Oklahoma summer with no air-conditioning. When Gary was home baby-sitting, he didn't allow anyone under the blanket except him.

Gary loved cereal, and he would go into the kitchen and fill up a huge bowl with a whole box of cereal and a half gallon of milk. He would then crawl back under the blanket to watch the TV. (He did this to drive Sharon and me nuts because that meant less cereal and milk for us.) All we could see was an army blanket with Gary's head sticking up under it. All we could hear was Gary's slurping noises drowning out the "Howdy Doody Show."

After years of such abuse and lots of jail time, Sharon and I decided it was time to retaliate. We had French glass doors at the back of the house. I rigged up a rope that Sharon could pull to slam the doors shut at just the right moment. She hid behind the door while I sneaked up behind the slurping hunk who was watching his favorite TV program and eating our cereal. On the way I picked up one of Dad's cowboy boots and hit him on the head as hard as I could. The slurping stopped and out from beneath the army blanket came the angriest, red faced, teary-eyed brother I have ever seen. Our plan was working.

I ran full speed toward the back of the house. Gary was right on my heels with outstretched arms. I passed through the glass French doors and, just as we had planned, Sharon sprung the trap. CRASH! Gary ran both arms through the glass. He cut his wrists so bad that every time his heart beat, blood squirted out. Gary probably would have bled to death, but it just so happened that our neighbor came by looking for a lost cow. He put all three of us in his car and we rushed Gary to an old country doctor in Collinsville. Sharon and I had mixed emotions. Though we were worried about Gary, we were glad to see that our trap had worked. The best part was watching Gary cry because the doctor didn't use anesthetic to put the numerous stitches in his arms. After we knew he was going to be all right, we laughed and laughed while doing jail time in the closet.

Being at home alone as much as we were meant that we ate whenever and whatever we wanted. About once a week, Dad went to the local grocery store located on the main intersection of our town. It was a strange store. It actually had dirt floors. The owner was a man with one leg, and the store was called Peg Leg Market. We always found him by just following the peg marks in the dirt. Dad did find some great buys at Peg Leg's. He bought cases of damaged canned goods. They were not damaged the way one would think; they just didn't have labels on the cans. He must have bought ten or twenty cases of these at a time, each large box labeled Corn, Peas, Spinach, Green Beans, and the food I hated most—Fruit Cocktail. Dad would take the cans out of the boxes and put them on the shelves in no order, so no one knew what was in each can. When I got hungry, I took down a can and shook it to try to determine its contents. After many shakes I might decide I had green beans, but it always turned out to be fruit cocktail.

Sometimes we ran completely out of food, and that was when we called our mother at her office. She didn't like this; in fact, it bothered her a lot. She was usually busy with a client or a new prospect. We didn't give up though. After numerous calls she finally got mad and headed our way. Gary, Sharon, and I ran upstairs and watched out the upstairs window for Mom's car; we could see across the prairie for miles. Eventually we saw a dust cloud with a small red dot in front. This would be mother in her fire-engine red Ford. We ran downstairs and out to the side of the road, usually just in time to see her drive by at seventy miles per hour. As she passed us, she would roll down the driver-side window and make a hook shot over the top of the car with a package of cinnamon rolls or some other packaged ready-to-eat snack. Through the years mother delivered many food items in this fashion, but cinnamon rolls were Gary's favorite. Since mother never looked back, she didn't see Gary catch the rolls in mid-air, take them out of the package, and lick off all the frosting. I think this was one of the reasons Gary became a great receiver for the high school football team. (I still won't eat cinnamon rolls.)

As Gary got older, we saw less and less of him around the farm. He hated farm work more than anyone I have ever known. He had an escape plan for every chore and might not show up again until dark. I think my parents finally got tired of chasing him. As Mother said, "Gary just won't dig." Gary was also crazy about girls. He fell in love with every girl he met. Some nights we had to go into town in order to drag him out of some girl's house. Even swollen rivers couldn't keep Gary away from one of his girlfriends. He'd sooner drown.

When Gary was fourteen and I was eleven, my parents bought him a motor scooter. Why, I don't know.

Maybe they thought he would run off with a girl and not come back. We worked on it all the time because it was in very bad condition when Dad bought it. We didn't have any modern tools, nor did Gary have the money to buy a tag for his scooter. One day we were eating a bowl of Wheaties and discovered that in each box of Wheaties cereal was a miniature replica of an automobile tag for a different state. Lucky for us, an Oklahoma car tag was one of the first tags we found. Though the tag was a lot smaller than a real car tag, it was almost the same size as an Oklahoma Motor Scooter Tag! We put it on the scooter and felt safe to take it on the highway.

One day while Gary was preoccupied with something else, I got on his motor scooter and headed to town. I noticed an Oklahoma Highway Patrolman parked on the side of the road up ahead, so I sat up straight and tried to look older. He pulled up behind me and turned on his red flashing light, so I pulled over to the side of the road. "Let me see your driver's license," he said.

"I'm sorry, but I don't have one," I replied. He pulled out his pad to write a ticket and walked to the back of the scooter to get my tag number.

"What the hell is Wheaties America?" he yelled. Lucky for me, he just shook his head and followed me home and told me if I was ever caught driving this scooter on the highway again he would take me to jail. I was very relieved he didn't give me a ticket. I guess I should have warned Gary, but I didn't.

We also saw less and less of Sharon as she started spending more time with her good friend Nancy. Nancy's father had died and Sharon helped her cope with the loss of her dad. Sharon was growing tired of the uncertainties in our life and the ups and downs in our parents' relationship. She also hated the farm and being isolated from town and her friends. Sharon was musically inclined like our mother and studied piano, the clarinet, and singing. When she was in the eleventh grade, she was named to the Oklahoma all-state band and voted band queen for Owasso High School.

For some reason that I don't understand, I had different feelings than Gary and Sharon did about our parents, our farm, and our animals. I felt it was my duty to keep my parents together and I often went back and forth talking to each one, trying to help them get along. I would worry about the animals, make sure they were fed and bedded down, and it was usually me who kept the fireplace going and clutter picked up in the house. I felt like my family needed me more than I needed them.

3

At Grandma's House

Occasionally our grandparents on our mother's side, the Calverts, would call and invite us to come to Tulsa for the weekend. I looked forward to these visits with glee. It was about time! At last I could live like a normal person. But these visits with my grandparents had their good and bad points. We had lots of great food to eat and personal attention, but instead of being able to come and go as we pleased (like it was at home in the wilderness) Grandma ruled with an iron hand. What a difference it was between no supervision at all and Grandma's absolute dictatorship. I know today that this is one of the reasons why my life has had so many ups and downs. I have never been in the middle of the road.

Grandma belonged to the Seventh Day Adventist Church. Gramps wasn't a member (because he chewed tobacco) but he never missed a church service. Their day of rest was the same as the Jewish Sabbath which starts at sundown Friday and lasts until sundown Saturday. This meant that Grandma and Gramps went to church on Saturday. They were not allowed to eat certain kinds of meat like ham; they had no alcohol, no make-up, no jewelry, no dancing, no low-cut dresses, no shorts, no movies, and no fun.

Grandma taught Bible lessons in people's homes in Tulsa and all around the state of Oklahoma. She brought hundreds of converts to the Adventist faith. Thirty years later when I was at the Tulsa Adventist Church with my grandmother, the preacher asked anyone who had studied the Bible with Sister Calvert to stand up. The church held four or five hundred people, and almost everyone stood up. At that time she was ninety years old and had taught free Bible studies since she was sixteen. Grandma had given seventy-four years of service to her faith. I was in awe.

Getting ready for the Sabbath on Friday was always busy. Grandma gave everyone chores to complete before sundown; all the washing and cleaning had to be done first. One of my jobs was to help with the laundry using a scrub board to wash the clothes. After the laundry was done, we all sat on the front porch to split peas and snap green beans. Then Grandma would prepare all the food for Friday night dinner, Saturday breakfast, and Saturday lunch, leaving the Sabbath day for worship and rest. A typical main dish was lentil patties with savita gravy. Savita was a soybean product used as a substitute for animal fat since Adventists were vegetarians. Accompaniments might be fresh green beans with no pork, a green salad, and Grandma's famous whole wheat bread. One of my fondest memories was the smell of Grandma's bread every Friday as it came out of the oven just before sundown. But beware! The minute the sun went down on Saturday, signaling the end of the Sabbath, we ran and hid to avoid more of Grandma's chores.

Since Grandma didn't drive, Gramps always drove her to all her evening Bible studies. He sat at home planning every one of these trips very carefully in order to avoid making any left-hand turns, making notes on a map with instructions. To my knowledge, Gramps never did make a left-hand turn.

I liked many things about my Grandma's house. I liked seeing people sitting on their front porch and the noise of family chatter coming out of open windows. I liked it that all the neighbors knew each other as well as each other's business. Probably my fondest memory of all was following the ice trucks making their deliveries to home owners that still had ice boxes. While kids ran barefooted on hot pavement behind an ice truck, the driver chipped off large pieces of ice and threw them to the kids. They were the forerunners of the ice cream trucks.

Gramps could hear us open the ice box from any room in the house. We tried to open it carefully and quietly, but he always heard us and hollered "Shut the damn ice box!" We loved to bug him. He even gave us lessons on the proper way to use an ice box. "First," he would say, "before you open the door, think and think what it is that you want. Then when you know for sure what it is you want, open it and grab it and then slam it shut." He was proud of his ability to get a jug of milk out and shut the door in less than one second. Today I understand why Gramps was so proud of his record—

the ice would melt if you stood there all day—but a few years later he was the same with his new gas refrigerator.

Grandma and Gramps lived on a dead end alley, and their small house faced Tulsa's Central Park. One of the park's attractions was a gathering place called the "park house" where the old folks could come to play cards and dominoes. Though Gramps was the type who acted pious, every now and then he would sneak over to the park house for a shot of whiskey. When he was really brave, willing to risk getting in trouble with Grandma, he went to the local restaurant to have ham and eggs, which was even worse than the whiskey. I enjoyed playing with my cars on the floor and watching Gramps sit in his chair listening to his radio programs. His chewing tobacco habit required a spit can on the floor beside his chair. He was very accurate and I never saw him miss. Grandma hated Gramps' tobacco chewing and told him often.

Gramps came to Oklahoma during the Oklahoma oil boom days and told us lots of interesting stories about these times. He was born in 1884 in Parkersburg, West Virginia to a very poor family. He had three brothers and a sister. To help his family, he quit school in the third grade and worked as a farm laborer. In his early teens, he befriended a country doctor who took a liking to him. Gramps accompanied him on all his house calls. The doctor was training him, and Gramps dreamed of becoming a doctor himself. This dream was soon shattered when his father was killed in a bar fight and he had to return to work to help his family. His older brother had a wife and family, but no money or job. They walked all the way from West Virginia to New Jersey, and after two months, they sent word that they had made it. Gramps never saw that brother again. A second brother, like his father, was also killed in a bar fight. The third brother and his sister headed to Oklahoma Indian Territory, but Gramps stayed behind to take care of his mother. He got a job working with a maintenance crew for the state prison outside of Parkersburg. One of my favorite stories that Gramps liked to tell was about a young prisoner who went down to the river with all the other prisoners in the dead of winter to ice skate for their exercise. Everyone laughed at him because he couldn't even stand up on his skates without falling down. After a few weeks, the guards figured he was the last one that might try to escape, so they got lazy about watching him. He waited for the right opportunity and one day shot off like a bullet, racing down the frozen river in expert fashion, never to be seen again!

Eventually Gramps got word from his brother that oil had been discovered in Oklahoma Indian Territory and jobs were plentiful. Gramps and his mother loaded up their belongings and moved to Big Heart, Oklahoma Indian Territory. The oil boom attracted men from all over wanting work, so gambling and prostitution flourished in the oil camps; it wasn't a good place to raise a family. They lived in a boarding house where at least twenty people sat around a large table to eat together. Gramps said that the man at the head of the table would have a tall stack of bread sitting in front of him. When the time came to eat, he would shout, "Okay! Time to deal the bread!" He proceeded to throw each piece of bread, Frisbee-style, around the table, making perfect throws to every single plate! Gramps made a living working for start-up oil companies and later became a field foreman for Barnsdall Oil Company, but he never gave up his dream to become a doctor.

Grandma's house was only a few blocks away from Tulsa's downtown business district with plenty of concrete on which to ride my tricycle. I missed riding my tricycle on the farm. One afternoon I decided it was time to see the city, so off I went on my trike, pedaling as fast as I could in rush hour traffic. I was having a great time until I realized I was lost. A policeman came to my rescue and asked me where I lived. I had no idea. To make matters worse, the only names I could remember were Grandma and Gramps. The policeman took me to the police station and fed me some ice cream. A few hours later my grandparents came to the station looking for a lost child. That was the last I saw of my tricycle.

Grandma's house was also only three blocks from the railroad tracks. Lying in bed at night, we could hear the trains working, the old steam engines chugging along, and lonely sounding whistles piercing the night air. Gary was crazy about trains, and it was amazing what all he knew about trains. He could tell you the route of every train and their time schedules. As we got a little older, after our grandparents were asleep, Gary and I would climb out the window and head to the tracks. The switch house was our first stop, where we visited with the workmen. Sometimes we would hitch a ride across town in a caboose. One time we even got to ride in the cab with the engineer.

The most exciting thing for me about the trains was going to hobo jungle. This was a place next to the railroad tracks where all the hobos met. It was in a woodsy area with lots of high grass and weeds. The hobos built campfires and cooked stew made from anything they could find. Their stories were very interesting to a young kid. Gary and I sat there listening and dreaming about being hobos and living on the rails.

There would always be at least one hobo who wanted to sell us a treasure map. They tricked us numerous times into going home to get them a dollar. When we gave one of them our dollar, he would say, "You stay here and I'll bring the map right back." Well, they never came back. One very convincing hobo drew me a map of the "real" location of the Old Lost Dutchman Mine in Arizona. I still have this map, and one of these days I may go take a look.

After spending the weekend in Tulsa with my grandparents, it was time to return to the farm. On the way home, I lay in the back window of our car so I could look up at the stars. This was years before seat belts, so all the kids liked to lie in the back window on the dash or simply crawl all over the car. My grandkids have no idea the fun they are missing in those neat little car seats. We were human missiles and didn't even know it.

"Colored town" was on the north side of downtown Tulsa; we drove through it in order to get home. It was never still. No matter what time of the day or night, the street was full of well-dressed, happy-looking people. I remember the black mannequins in the neat store front windows, the interesting smells, and the music of a world I knew nothing about.

It was not until many years later that I realized what an injustice was done to these fellow Americans. Just think what it was like to be black in the 1940's and 1950's. They couldn't stay in a hotel or go into a restaurant. Black people had to go to the back door and be served in the kitchen or else eat out on the back steps. They were forced by law to use separate drinking fountains and restrooms. They had to ride in the back of the bus and they always stepped off the sidewalk if they met a white person coming their way. The bus and train depots even had separate waiting rooms and boarding areas for whites and blacks. It was impossible for a black man to get a good job except as a shoe shine boy or a janitor. If I had been born black, I think I would have belonged to the Black Panthers or some other militant group. It just wasn't right.

One night our family was leaving the outskirts of Tulsa after a weekend visit with my grandparents. We followed the old narrow highway that led to the wilderness through a dark and heavy fog. I almost fell asleep. All of a sudden I became aware that my parents were having a heated argument. They were either madly in love or hated each other; there was no in between. Dad stopped the car on this scary road, got out, and slammed the car door. My mother slid over into the driver's seat and, as she drove off, I saw my dad slowly disappear in the fog through the rear window. In a burst of panic, Gary, Sharon, and I screamed at our mother and begged her to go back. She did. In only a few moments, our fear and despair changed to relief and loving happiness. This memory and the terror I felt while watching Dad disappear in the fog will always be with me. I wanted to save him, like a person slowly sinking under water.

4

The Fulbrights and the Sherrills

Besides my Grandmother and Grandfather Calvert, I had two other sets of grandparents. I shall explain. When my dad was born in Arkansas, his mother, my Grandmother Fulbright, died during childbirth. The Sherrills were distant cousins and lived a few miles down the creek. They had just lost a baby, so were excited to take in a new baby for a short time. After a year went by, Granddad Fulbright remarried and told the Sherrills that he was ready to come and retrieve his son. That night the Sherrills packed up everything they owned and moved from Arkansas to El Campo, Texas, approximately six hundred miles away. They didn't bring Dad back to visit his real father until ten years later. Out of respect for the Sherrills, Dad took their name even though his birth certificate says Fulbright.

The greatest trip that I ever took with my family was to Arkansas to visit my Granddad Fulbright and my father's real brothers and sisters. To me this was the ultimate adventure. The Ozark Mountains were beautiful and the people were the friendliest people I'd ever met. The trees and winding clear streams were such a change from the prairies of Oklahoma. It took two hard days of traveling to reach the point where we turned off the main highway. The highways in the late forties were narrow with no shoulders, and all the bridges were one lane. We also drove through every town; bypasses had not been thought of yet. Our tube tires caused us at least two flats each one-way trip, and since there were no fences on the open range, cattle would often be standing on the road. With no motels or chain restaurants, every overnight stay and every meal was an adventure in itself.

To adults and kids alike, the most terrifying places on the highway were the bridges. The bridge over the Arkansas River was a mile long and had just enough room for one car going in one direction. It was rusty and had a wood floor. The bridge over the White River was only a few blocks long and also of wood construction, but it was a swinging bridge two or three hundred feet above the river. I never saw this bridge because, out of fear, I would get on the floor with my mother, brother, and sister. As dad slowly drove over this swinging bridge, I can still remember the sound it made, but once we crossed it we were closer to the Fulbright farm.

At last we saw the sign that said seventy-five miles to Batesville. We turned off the main highway and continued along a gravel road. Suddenly Dad stopped and looked both to the right and to the left. We were in the middle of a creek! He pointed downstream and said his parents' farm was a few miles that way. We left the dirt road and drove the rest of the way in the creek.

Finally we made it. On the side of this beautiful creek was a small neat shack with rocking chairs on the front porch and a tin roof. It looked like something out of a movie. As we drove out of the creek bed, Dad started honking his horn. Out ran my grandparents and a bunch of aunts, uncles, and cousins. They made us feel like kings!

My dad's brother Harry had a beautiful ranch a few miles from the Fulbrights. Dad would have traded everything he owned for Uncle Harry's farm. It had a beautiful creek that flowed year round and the grass grew up to the bellies of his fat and healthy Black Angus cattle. One day we asked Uncle Harry if we could go for a swim in the creek. He warned us that early in the year the water was too cold, but this didn't stop my newfound cousins and me. Well, cold wasn't the word. It was freezing. My private parts disappeared.

Uncle Harry was a lot of fun. He played jokes on everyone and could sing and play a guitar. He was six feet two inches tall and probably weighed three hundred pounds. My family said that I looked a lot like Uncle Harry because of our round heads and very short legs. (In fact today I'm only five foot nine, but I am the tallest person I know sitting down.)

I thought old Granddad Fulbright was a cranky, cruel farmer; he looked and acted mean. Every day he got so mad at his cows, he chased them all over the Ozarks, beating them half to death when he caught them. He had an impressive garden and used a mule to pull his plow.

At night when we were trying to go to sleep, we could hear all the noises of the mountains. The scariest was the screaming of the mountain lions that walked the high ridges. With no electricity at the farm, the gas lights added an extra excitement to the night. The air in the Ozark Mountains smelled sweet, and at night, as we looked up to the heavens, it looked like home; every star was there. My Granddad built a wooden flume from a spring about a quarter of a mile from the cabin. It wound through the trees and right into the kitchen window. When we wanted water we just opened the small wooden door and spring water would run into the sink. On Saturday morning it was time for church. We loaded up in a wagon and went to town. This was a short trip of about two miles. Strangely everyone in this town was related to me. My dad's parents were also Seventh Day Adventists. The small white church fit in perfectly with the beautiful Ozark Mountains.

That night after sundown, we made homemade ice cream under the stars. I thought I was in heaven. When it was time to leave, Granddad started crying and begged us not to go. He gave Dad an old trailer which we hooked up to our car to carry the horse, cow, and pig Granddad had given us. As we drove off, I looked back and wished we could see them more often.

The trip home with the horse, cow, and pig was a nightmare. It was late summer, so hot the animals nearly died of thirst. Their tongues were sticking out and foam was coming from their mouths. Every few miles we stopped at a service station to borrow a hose to water them down. Finally, early in the morning with the sun just coming up, we drove in to our farm. Dad backed the trailer up to the gate and let the horse and cow out. The pig just fell out. Probably half razorback, it jumped up and headed south in a full run back to Arkansas. We never saw the pig again. The horse and cow lived for years. We made this trip to Arkansas four more times before Granddad Fulbright died. He was eighty-five years old and was found dead in his garden.

I don't know as much about my Sherrill grandparents because we didn't see them as often. I do know that they moved from El Campo, Texas to Shreveport, Louisiana. My Granddad Sherrill made brooms for a living and traveled from town to town selling them. I also know that he had a pet parakeet that he loved. We have a picture of him holding his bird up next to his mouth, allowing it to clean his teeth!

5

First Friends

Our mother told us over and over to be choosy about our friends. Living in the wilderness like we did with very few kids nearby, we didn't have much to choose from. Most of them could have played the part of the banjo player in the movie *Deliverance*. One kid named Bob lived about a mile and a half away, just across a mung bean field. We met by accident one morning on the bus when the bus driver swerved to miss a dog in the road. I fell on top of Bob—one of the most dangerous kids in the world—and he became my first friend.

In Bob's defense, his dad was too strict and should have been put in jail for child abuse. Even though Bob lived over a mile away, some nights I could hear his screams. His dad would tie him up in the barn and whip him. Bob often showed me cuts and black and blue marks on his back, legs, and buttocks. This undoubtedly had a profound effect on him. When I walked over to his house, I could always find him in his dad's workshop making some type of weapon to injure or kill something or someone.

One afternoon I found him in the work shop sharpening a butcher knife. We went outside and were chasing each other around his outhouse. Not knowing that he had picked up a brick, I turned and ran toward him. He hit me in the mouth, breaking two large pieces out of my front buckteeth. We desperately tried to find the pieces so we could glue them back in, but a chicken got to them first and ate them. I hid my damaged teeth for days, but finally my parents noticed. If a kid had a bad overbite in the 1940's and 1950's, he just had to live with it, and unfortunately I had one. People called me "Bucky Beaver" and "Snaggle Tooth." One joke was that I could eat corn through a picket fence. After Bob hit me in the face with a brick, it was even worse. My school pictures that year were so bad I couldn't pay kids to take one. This affected me for years. I didn't smile in a picture until I married my wife Pat some twenty-five years later.

Bob did come over to my house later to say he was sorry for knocking my teeth out and I accepted his apology. As he was leaving, he grabbed a can of gas and started emptying it all over our house. I couldn't believe it! I had to stop him from lighting a match. I could never understand Bob. On several occasions he tried to set our house on fire. One time a friend of my mother's came over and was in the outhouse. Bob went out and opened the door and began throwing lit kitchen matches on her. She ran out screaming. Walking down the road with Bob was also a problem. If he wasn't throwing rocks at cars, he was throwing lit matches in the grass. I frantically put them out just in time for him to throw another and another.

Every year our school had Western Days. We dressed up like cowboys, and some of the older kids even brought horses. I decided I would be an Indian, so I put a chicken feather in my hair and tied two wash cloths together that barely covered my skimpy little underwear. The minute I got off the bus, my teacher sent me to the principal's office. They were going to call my parents, but I was in luck. Bob's mother was there to pick him up for shooting a kid in the back with a homemade arrow.

One day Bob told me that he had found a great way to make money. Together we began collecting pop bottles and turning them into the Peg Leg Market for a penny each. Peg Leg kept all the bottles we sold out behind his store. When he wasn't watching, we put the same bottles we had sold him into our little red wagon and took them up the street to the drug store and sold the drug store owner another twenty-five cents worth. To our amazement, he also put his bottles out back. We loaded them up again and headed back to Peg Leg's. This was great! We laughed every time we made the trip. But then we got greedy. Why walk back and forth? We could sell them to the same place over and over. This turned out to be too fast. Peg Leg caught on and called our parents. I should have asked Bob where he got the wagon because he had stolen it too.

When school started the next fall, I thought I was making progress when I made a couple of normal friends—Jimmy and Mike. Both Jimmy and Mike lived in town, giving me a chance to sometimes stay in town after school. Jimmy had a few problems like the rest of us, but this just helped him to fit in. His dad made Jimmy pay rent. He would work after school at the cafe washing dishes, and he had a morning paper route. He loved to gamble. He once lost his dad's house to me in a poker game, but his dad refused to give me the title. Jimmy had a very bad temper. I soon learned that he would go nuts if he didn't get his way. No matter what it was, Jimmy always thought he was better than everyone else at running, eating, or drinking, though he never won when put to a contest.

Mike was also a normal acting kid. I asked our teacher if I could change chairs so I could get to know him. Everything was going smoothly until I noticed Mike showing something to the girls sitting next to him. I took a closer look and it looked like he had his penis in his pocket! After class I followed him to the restroom and asked him where he had gotten it. He showed me his trick. He had cut a hole in his pocket lining and just pulled himself out. Noticing how all the girls giggled, I thought this might be something I should try. That night I cut a hole in my pocket and pulled as hard as I could, but I could not get mine to show. This was my first realization that all boys are not the same length.

Years later Mike was caught doing a new trick. He took a date to the movies. He cut a hole in the bottom of his popcorn box and stuck his penis in the hole. While his date watched the movie she reached in the box for some popcorn. When she realized what she had grabbed, she screamed for the manager. The next day at school I looked for Mike. I noticed a bunch of kids in a circle. This usually meant a fight, but this time it was Mike down on the ground showing all the guys how to fuck! He had made a hole in the ground and lined it with cotton and was actually hard and in the ground! About that time a teacher grabbed him and he was missing from school for a couple of weeks. Years later Mike became a horticulturist.

I have fond memories of several people in our community who helped me make friends. One was my Little League coach. He had an old 1940 Ford and he would load all of the town boys and our equipment in his car and take us from town to town to play baseball. Like today, many people like him work hard to help young kids. We only won one game in three years, but we still had fun. That one game was the final game of my last season playing baseball. Coach loaded us up in his car and we arrived at the baseball field and started to practice, but the other team didn't show up. We won by forfeit, and Coach jumped up and down with joy. He was so excited that he stopped on the way home at a Tasty Freeze and treated us to all the ice cream we could eat. I went to bed happy that night because at last we had won our first game. The next morning we found out that Coach had taken us to the wrong baseball field.

One of my friends on the baseball team was Cleo. He was a good baseball player and could run very fast. He was also known as a "leaper." Like many other small towns, ours had a water tower that was probably sixty feet tall. At the base of the water tower, the city stored sand and gravel. The sand pile was huge—about ten feet high and twenty feet wide. Cleo dared anyone to climb up to the first level on the tower and jump into the sand. The first level was roughly twenty feet above the sand pile. This was great fun because we would sink into the sand up to our waists. One day after school, we all went down to the tower. Cleo had been bragging all day that he was going to jump from the second level, approximately a forty foot jump. Cleo went slowly up the ladder to the second level and stood on the steel girder looking down at us. We yelled, "Jump! Jump! Jump!"

Cleo leaped off the tower screaming, "Geronimo!" He missed the sand pile and landed on the concrete, breaking all the bones in both feet.

6

Animal Farm

My parents loved all animals and neither of them would hurt a fly. I remember us stopping on the highway many times heading home to help a turtle off its back. I couldn't understand why Dad invited some friends to come to our farm to go duck hunting. We all loaded up and headed for one of our ponds where we had spotted some Canadian Geese. This was really quite fun. We got down on our hands and knees downwind from any unsuspecting duck, crawled quietly up the pond dams, and then jumped up ready to shoot. Dad fired and got one. All his friends bragged about his great shot and we rushed over to retrieve the large bird. To our amazement, the goose was not dead.

"Shoot it again! Shoot it again!" Dad's friends yelled. Dad would not shoot and he would not let anyone else shoot either. Instead we carried the goose home. It lived in my parent's bedroom with a wing splint for about three weeks. We were able to release this beautiful bird to nature. As we watched it soar up in the air to join its flock, I knew Dad would never shoot anything again. For over forty years, I have watched the wild ducks and geese heading south, and this memory always comes to mind.

Of all the animals on our farm, we loved our dogs most. We raised and showed registered Collies. My parents dreamed of having beautiful kennels full of show dogs, so we went into business. The only problem with our business was we didn't have enough money for the proper kennels. In fact, we didn't even have the money for dog food.

We started out with three female Collies and one male. Without pens or fences, the dogs ran wild and the three females got pregnant at the same time. A few months later three litters were born. We now had approximately thirty loose dogs. One of the litters was born under the house. Dad forced Gary and me to go after that litter of pups because, he said, he was too big to fit through the small opening to the crawl space. Spiders and snakes were also known to emerge from beneath the house. For some forgotten reason, Gary and I began to fight in this narrow space under the house. Dad leaned down and yelled, "You son-of-a-bitches—you better stop it!"

"How are you going to stop us?" we hollered back laughing.

"I'll show you!" he said and he began to launch baseball-sized rocks at us from outside the opening. I couldn't believe my dad was throwing rocks at us! Next I heard my brother cry out in pain. He'd been hit. Gary gave up and crawled out of the hole. Just as he reached the opening, I saw my Dad's hand land a karate chop on the back of Gary's neck. Then he grabbed him and rolled him out into the grass. I was next. I decided to spend the night with the pups.

Having all these pups around didn't seem to matter much until they were about ten weeks old. If anyone tried to go outside they risked being attacked by a horde of piranha-like pups. They would tear a person to shreds with their razor sharp teeth. The only way to get to the car or school bus was to call the pups from our back door. As they raced around to the back, we ran out the front—usually making it to the car or bus just in time. When it was time to feed, we threw some food out the door and watched the feeding frenzy. Finally after a few months, we were able to give away all the pups, and things somewhat returned to normal.

My parents never reached their goal of operating a prestigious dog kennel, so their next endeavor was to have a successful cattle operation. One morning I was awakened by the sound of two large cattle trucks pulling into our farm. Dad had made what he called "an excellent buy" for one hundred head of half Hereford and half Texas Longhorn cows. The cattle had supposedly come from a huge ranch in New Mexico, but the trucks had Mexican license plates. Ranches in that part of the country were often as many as 100,000 acres, and they had no crossroads or fences. These cows were lean, mean, and wild.

As the trucks drove off, we watched the whole herd of new cows running as fast as they could to the other end of our farm, which was approximately one mile from the house. When they reached the fence they didn't stop; they just turned around and ran all the way back. They were so used to wide open space and no fencing that they went crazy. Dad was getting worried. "Stop them", he yelled and shoved me toward the field. How in the hell was I supposed to stop a herd of a hundred wild cows?

Sometime later that night the cows finally gave out and stopped. "I'll never get the body fat back on those cows," Dad said. "Every time they gain a pound they run off two."

"They act more like greyhounds to me," I said under my breath.

That weekend Dad wanted to spray the cattle for flies and ticks. He told Gary and me to stand by the entrance gate to the corral. He went down to drive the cows up and around the barn. Our job was to wave our arms and turn them into the corral. Gary was looking for any way to escape. I begged him to stay. He agreed to help me get the cows in the corral and then he'd run for town. As this large herd came around the corner, they spotted us, lowered their heads, and charged right by us. Dad was furious. He cussed us and the cows and told Gary and me to bring the cows back around the barn. Picking up a big stick, he said, "I'll show you how to turn'um."

Gary and I had to walk about a mile to get behind the cows again. "Let's stampede them," I said to Gary. Not being very happy with this job, Gary agreed. We yelled and threw rocks at the cows, which also got the dogs excited. It didn't take much. The cows turned the corner around the barn and headed straight for Dad at full speed, bellowing, farting, and kicking their back feet in the air. Dad barely escaped being trampled.

"You didn't turn'um," I said. He'd have killed Gary and me if he'd caught us.

We had kept the old, male dog Laddy that had been the lone sire of all the pups, but Laddy was just not meant to live on a farm. He didn't understand farm life. He would chase our cows all day long. Dad said that if Laddy didn't stop chasing the cows, he was going to have to get rid of him. One day old Lad was chasing a cow and grabbed on by its tail and bit it off. So delighted with his accomplishment, he went after another and another. That night when Dad came home, I thought he was going to have a stroke. Most of his cows were now bobtailed. Old Lad finally went too far one day. He was chasing a tractor with a side sickle for cutting weeds and got his front leg caught in the sickle. We tried to take care of him the best we could, but his leg never healed and he died a few months later.

This solved one of Dad's problems, but he still worried about our cows. I was surprised to find him at home one day when I came home from school. He looked depressed. He told me he was so busy at work he didn't have the time to take care of the cows. He was desperate. The fences needed work, the cows were not being fed on time, and winter was closing in. He was scared they would all die if we had one of our bad winters. Of course Gary was nowhere around. Dad asked me if I thought I was ready for the responsibility to take over. I was excited and proud that Dad thought I was old enough to do the job. He even made me a deal.

"Son, if you get these cows through the winter and this spring, I'll give you half the profit we make." This was all I needed, that extra incentive to really work hard. All winter long I put in many hard hours of work, never missing a feeding and fixing the fences and keeping the ice broken on the ponds.

As Dad had feared, that winter was one of the coldest on record. Our lake froze solid. We had put some ducks on the lake to provide constant movement in the water in hopes this wouldn't happen. This particular night, however, the ducks just couldn't do the job. The cows were dying of thirst, bellowing at the top of their lungs. It was quite a sight to see them bellowing all at once with their breath steaming in the cold night air.

Dad and I headed down to the lake with picks in hand. The cows went with us. We could not swing the picks because the cows were all over us. Dad said, "Let's drive the cows to the corral and lock them up." After an hour or so the cows were securely locked in the corral and, at last, we had plenty of room to swing our picks. We broke through the ice and the water rushed up through the new opening. The cows must have smelled the fresh water. They went crazy and broke out of the corral—all one hundred or so stampeded to the lake! Dad yelled at me to quickly move out to the center of the lake in order to escape the stampede. The only problem was the cows were running so fast that when they hit the ice, they slid out into the middle of the lake with us! There they were, staring at us, waiting for direction. It was strangely quiet and then CRACK! The ice broke. Dad, the cows, and I were then swimming together in deep, freezing water. Dad screamed, "Grab a cow's tail!" Lucky for us, old Lad hadn't gotten them all. So we held on and the cows slowly pulled us to safety. By the time we made it home, approximately a half a mile away, our clothes were frozen solid. I had lost my shoes and my feet were blue. We managed to survive, but Dad never regained feeling in his toes.

Probably the hardest thing I did that winter was to shoot a cow. I think cows may be the dumbest animals in the world. If one falls down or gets knocked down by another cow, sometimes it will just lie there and die. No matter how hard you try to get it up, it refuses to try. After days of lying on the ground, the animal gets sores that start to rot. The most humane thing to do is to destroy it; if you don't, it can suffer for days. The vet told me the best place to shoot a cow was in the head, but I could hardly bear to do that. The cow looks up at you with those big, sad, brown eyes.

I should have known better, but I asked my friend Bob to come over and give me some help. He loved it. "Let's give them a chance," he said. Bob took all the bullets out except one and spun the chamber of the gun around and then pulled the trigger. Every time the gun clicked, the cow blinked. We traded the gun back and forth until one of us shot the cow. We later called this game "Cow Roulette."

Before I knew it, spring had arrived and I had kept my part of the deal. Dad and I loaded up the newly born calf crop and a few older mother cows and headed to the sale barn. We were in luck because cattle prices were up and it looked like we were going to make a profit. Dad was counting our money. "Don't forget our deal," I said. "Where's my half?"

"Son, I'm going to make you an even better deal. If I ever get in that kind of situation again, I'll give you all the profit." I should have listened to Grandma Calvert. A few years earlier she'd said Dad had shafted her on a cow deal. I learned what shaft means.

To support the cattle operation, we also had horses. I wanted to learn how to ride, but horseback riding on our farm was not like being at a dude ranch. First I had to catch a horse, and this was no easy matter. My first strategy was to get a rope and a bucket of feed and head for the far corner of the farm. I could see the horses standing there with their tails swatting flies and their hind legs hiked up ready to kick. They watched and waited for me to walk almost a mile, and then, just as I was ready to put the rope around one of the mare's neck, they all ran like hell to the other end of the pasture. After several failed attempts and miles of walking, I eventually figured out how to catch them. I hid behind the pond dam and waited for them to come for a drink. As they were bent over drinking, I ran up behind them waving and screaming and scared them into the pond. Once the horses were in the pond, it was a snap! I could jump in and swim over to the horse I wanted to ride and climb on. As it swam toward shore, I grabbed its long mane of hair and held on tight. Once it emerged from the water, I was in for a wild ride.

With no saddle or bridle, the horse went where it wanted to go at top speed. We had some persimmon trees that had low limbs and, as the horse got smarter, it would head for these trees. If I didn't jump off in a hurry, I was raked off by these branches. If this didn't work, the horse would fall down and roll over me. One hot afternoon I was sitting on the roof of the barn watching the horses slowly walk by. All of a sudden I had a great idea. I would jump from the barn onto the horse's back. This worked great except that I had left the gate open. After landing on this plug's back, it took off down the road at top speed for a mile and then suddenly bolted and turned in front of our neighbor's driveway. I sailed over the horse's head and landed on my back in the gravel, losing most of the skin on my back in the process.

The neighbors ran out and took me to the same doctor that had treated my brother after the glass door incident. The doctor turned a fan on my back and said, "This might burn a little." He then dumped a mixture of iodine and alcohol on my back and cleaned out the gravel pieces. The painful agony this caused was ample motivation to learn how to use a bridle.

The following summer was as hot as the previous winter had been cold. Our pasture was unable to support the amount of cattle we had. To compensate Dad made a deal with a rancher about twenty miles from our house. This rancher had over two thousand fenced acres located in rough and rugged land that ran alongside the Verdigris River. In this part of Oklahoma, this was about the only place you could find trees and dense underbrush. Our only problem was getting the cows to the new ranch.

A truck driver came over and gave Dad a quote to load and haul the cattle to their new pasture. "Forget it," Dad said. "I'll drive the sons-of-a-bitches before I'll pay that much!" So the great cattle drive was about to begin. All the neighbor kids heard about the cattle drive and wanted to help. By now I knew how to ride, but it still took us one whole day to catch the horses. We had about ten kids on horseback ready to go, plus Gary and me and our trail master, Dad. We could hardly wait for the sun to come up.

We thought that by using the county road with fences on both sides, we could keep the cattle under control. We cautioned the neighbors to keep their gates closed. Two kids were standing guard at their gate, but their efforts were not sufficient to stop a herd of cows hell bent on taking a detour. All the cows and thirteen horses chasing them ran through their garden. Dad paid them for the damages and the drive headed on. Everything was looking good; we had made great time and we were over halfway there. Taking our time not to run the cows in the heat of the day, we were feeling good.

All of a sudden, this guy drove up behind us and started honking his truck horn. The cows stampeded and ran down the road at full speed. This nut, trying to get by and persistently honking his horn, ran them for over a mile. By the time we caught up, a couple of the cows had died in the heat. The other cows and our horses were in bad shape and needed water. A mile or so up the road were some old coal pits that were always full of water. As soon as our horses got a whiff, they took off and the cows followed. I laughed when Dad's horse threw him on the road before he reached the pits. At last all the animals had their bellies full, and it was time to attempt the final distance, but the cows had other ideas. They weren't going anywhere. Every time we got them back on the road heading in the right direction, they turned and ran back to the coal pits. It was dark by the time we got them out and finally arrived at the new ranch. As we slowly headed home on our horses, we laid back and looked up at the stars, singing songs and dreaming of being real cowboys.

The next morning we got the bad news. In the darkness we had put the cows in the wrong pasture, and this ranch had no fences. We spent the rest of the summer looking for our cows in the thick underbrush of the river bottom. We found about half of them by the end of the summer. That fall our remaining small herd was moved back by truck. I wished we hadn't found any of them.

The summer after that, Dad took on a hired hand to help with the cattle and crops. He also gave him complete control of Gary and me. As far as Gary and I were concerned, he was a taskmaster from hell. Dad had decided to plant forty acres of sugarcane on part of our farm. We were in the process of cutting sugarcane, and of course we didn't use any modern tractors or equipment like most of the farmers used in our area. Instead we used hand sickles like they used in the Old Testament. One afternoon our taskmaster caught us jumping on the neat stacks of sugarcane. He picked up one and whipped us good. This was not going to work;

we had to get him fired. Gary had hidden his motor scooter in the cane field for a later planned escape. When the taskmaster turned his back, Gary and I made a run for the scooter. On the way to town to tell Mother we'd been beaten half to death, we hit some loose gravel and turned the scooter over. With these new cuts and bruises, our story of a beating really worked. The taskmaster was history. Dad didn't give up on the cattle operation though. A few years later, he started raising Herefords.

7

Sex Education

My sex education began when I was quite young while visiting Grandma and Gramps in Tulsa. I loved to go to a nearby park and play in the sand. Gary had made some friends, and one of his new friend's little sister Mary was playing in the sand box. Little Mary was very quiet and shy, so it surprised me when she said, "If you show me yours, I'll show you mine." I had no idea what she was talking about. So I asked, "Show you what?" She pointed to my private area. This really scared me.

I knew something was wrong with that area because one time when I was lying on my back relaxing in the bathtub, Grandma walked in, saw me, and screamed, "Cover up!" Then she threw a wash cloth over my privates. When she left the room, I lifted the cloth and took a peek. It looked just the same.

So no way would I show little Mary, but instead, I said I would draw it in the sand. I drew a pretty good picture and then it was her turn. She reached over and just made a hole in the sand. Then she laughed real big and got up and ran. I stayed there for some time trying to figure this out. It was starting to get dark so I headed for Grandma's house. I noticed up the path that my brother and little Mary's brother were standing with a rope in their hands. When I got to them, they grabbed me and tied me to a park bench. Then they got some sticks and started beating me. "Have you been fucking little Mary?" they yelled. I didn't know what they were talking about. They just kept repeating over and over, "Have you been fucking little Mary?" I was getting tired of being whipped with sticks, so I cried out, "Yes, yes, yes!" After that they untied me and told me not to ever do it again. I promised and went on to Grandma's house, and when I got there, I asked her what fucking meant. I thought I was going to get killed. She never told me, but whatever it meant, I'm never going to do it.

My sex education continued when I started riding the school bus. Once I overheard some older boys on the bus talking about their sexual adventures. One story stuck in my mind and affected me later in life. "Once you get inside a girl you can't stop, no matter what," one guy said and continued to explain. "I was having sex with a girl and her parents walked in. I couldn't stop and had to finish in front of them. We were just like dogs—we got hung up!" I believed this guy because I had seen dogs get "hung up;" I knew this to be a fact. For years I did not want to try anything with a girl.

A few weeks after the dog story, I heard a different boy say that every time a boy masturbated, his semen would turn into a baby. The only protection was to clean up every drop and flush it down the stool. I had dreams at night that hundreds of babies were under my bed. My grandma didn't help either. She told me if I ever did things like that, I would go to hell and be blind when I got there. But that wasn't the worst of it. Grandma was so worried about us touching ourselves that she would sneak in the bedroom while we were asleep, carefully pull back the covers, and smell our fingers. Grandma had nostrils as large as chicken eggs. Gramps always said, "When I first met her, she picked her nose with a hair pin. Now she can cram her whole damn fist in." After many nights of having Grandma lift my hand out from under the covers, I felt it was time to give her a surprise. While waiting for her bed check, I put my index finger up to the knuckle in my rectum. When she pulled back the covers and lifted my hand to her face, she almost vomited. That was the last time I was ever bed checked.

Our farm was also a good source of information. One spring afternoon I arrived home on the school bus and headed to the barn to feed the cows. One of the cows had given birth to a new calf a few days earlier. When I got to the barn, I watched this calf suck its mother. It made me wonder. No one was around, so I dropped my pants and shuffled over to the calf. I grabbed the calf's nose and pushed it toward my penis. To my surprise that calf grabbed me so quickly and sucked so hard that I couldn't get loose. I was in real trouble! Not only could I not get loose, the calf was now bucking its head, trying to get milk. Then Dad walked into the barn. That was my first and last sex with any farm animal.

My first real human girlfriend was Lena Bell. She was a little older than me and about six inches taller. I really had a bad case of puppy love. Lena Bell and I went to all the grade school events, one of these being the Picnic Box Auction. In the gym all the girls fixed up fancy picnic boxes containing enough food for two, and the boys bid on them, one at a time. The highest bidder of each box got to sit together with its owner and share the dinner. Lena Bell was good-looking and popular. I had to spend every dime I had to outbid the other boys.

We dated three or four years and had lots of fun together. One beautiful night I went to her home and knocked on the screen door. I was beginning to have strong sexual feelings for Lena Bell and we had not even kissed in all these years. It was time for some action. She came to the door and stood there in front of me. She looked so good even through the dirty screen door separating us. "I think after three or four years of going steady, it's time that we at least start kissing, and maybe other things," I told her. She agreed and told me to wait at the door. I was really getting excited thinking about what might happen after our first hot kiss. Then without warning, she threw a pan of dishwater through the screen and slammed the door! "I guess this means we're through," I said aloud to myself, standing there soaking wet. A couple of months later she got married.

At last I met a girl named Margo who I thought might be good for kissing. She was real cute and a good athlete. The only problem was that she had a bad overbite—buck teeth like mine. We were good friends and had lots of fun on dates. One weekend her church was having a hay ride and she asked me to go. That night a full moon shone on Margo's lovely lips as she lay on her back in the hay. I couldn't stand it. I had to kiss her. I leaned over slowly and carefully. Just as my lips were about to touch hers, the wagon hit a bump and my buck teeth hit hers. We were both embarrassed and just held hands the rest of the trip.

That night I asked Gary for some advice on kissing. I figured he had plenty of expertise. He told me to practice on my pillow at night and to open my mouth real wide. A few days later it was time to try to kiss Margo again. She was still thinking about the last time, so when I reached over to kiss her, she shut her eyes and held her lips tightly closed covering her teeth. I moved in with my eyes closed and mouth wide open, taking in, not just her mouth, but her nose and chin. We broke up.

I don't think young people had much preparation for sex back in the fifties because people didn't talk about sex. You just got in a car with your date and parked on some lonely road and kissed for hours. Having sex before marriage was practically impossible because of the clothes the girls wore—cancans, layer upon layer of starched petticoats. By the time you worked your way through all these undergarments, you lost interest.

I always wondered if girls ever noticed me trying to take off their bra. I took one of my sister's bras and put it around a tree to practice getting it off with one hand, but put it on some hot babe and I was all thumbs. I spent hours one time fumbling on a girl's back trying to undo her bra while kissing and acting like I was doing nothing. At the same time, she sat there acting like she didn't feel a thing. At last after numerous attempts, her bra shot loose. We were both in shock. She went in the house with her bra undone leaving us both still virgins.

I was getting desperate for sex, so I turned to one of the so-called "easy girls." She was the one Grandma told me had hot pants. As I worked my way through her starched petticoats, and layer after layer came off faster than normal, I noticed two things that night. One, this girl was helping me take things off, and two, a strange odor became stronger and stronger as each layer came off. By the time I was within sight of her panties, I noticed they were embroidered in blue with a day of the week—Tuesday—and it was Friday. With quick thinking, I told "Hot Pants" that I had to stop, that I respected her too much to go any further. She thought I was the nicest boy she had ever met.

One hot summer afternoon a friend invited my friend Ronnie and me to his house. He had just talked to a prostitute and she was coming over to his house for twenty dollars! Ronnie and I didn't want to have any part in this, so he told us we could hide in the closet and watch. We agreed. We left the closet door cracked just enough to see. In a few minutes the two of them came into the bedroom. Our friend looked at us and made a face. We were stuffing clothes in our mouths trying not to laugh out loud.

She was a big girl, probably weighing two-hundred pounds. Our friend stood there naked and ready to go. They had already started to sweat in this hot and humid room. Before she lay down, she mentioned that she was having her monthly period and suggested they put a newspaper on the bed to keep from soiling his bedspread. Our friend agreed, but the only reading material that was ever in his room was the funny papers.

They carefully spread the comics out on the bed and she lay on top of them. He gave us one more look at the closet and climbed on. A couple of minutes went by and he was finished and headed for the bathroom. She got up to get dressed and the paper had stuck to her backside. She bent over to peel the funny papers off her rump, revealing a perfect imprint of Dick Tracy. We couldn't stifle our laughter. She chased us out of the house threatening murder. Our friend refused to pay her and she left in a huff. Later that night she called his dad and told him his son owed her twenty dollars. His dad made him pay.

After years of sharing a bedroom with my brother Gary, I finally got my own bedroom. Our house had a breezeway between the garage and the house and at one end of the breezeway was an old hand-dug well. This breezeway, water well and all, became my bedroom when my mother remodeled our house. The unusual thing about my bedroom addition was that my parents did not fill in the well. It was four feet wide and thirty feet deep. I could pull the floor boards up out of my closet and show all my friends the bottomless pit beneath! The best thing about my new room was that I was the only person downstairs. I had a window open at all times with no screen, so I could come and go as I pleased. When friends came by, they crawled in the window to visit. Otherwise I left with them to roam the night looking for fun things to do.

Walking the main highway in hopes of hitching a ride was our favorite. If by chance we were picked up, we rode a few miles and then asked to get out. Then we walked across the highway and hitched another ride back home. One night my friend Jim came over and we headed down to the highway. We were thrilled when two girls picked us up. I remembered what my grandmother had said, "Watch out for girls with hot pants, smokers, and NEVER hang around with girls from West Tulsa." My heart started beating rapidly when I realized these girls were smokers and acted like they had hot pants. I asked them where they were from, and boy! were we in luck—WEST TULSA.

After a few moments of driving, the girls suggested we play "Seven Minutes in Heaven." We agreed without knowing what the game was. I got in the back seat and one girl started kissing me. I soon learned the game. For seven minutes we kissed on the mouth without stopping. Her lips and breath were hot from smoking and I was having some hot feelings. These West Tulsa girls made up for all the kisses I had missed from my first girlfriend, Lena Bell, as well as all the others.

After kissing for hours, the West Tulsa girls took us home and kicked us out of their car. They said we were too young and they didn't want to go to jail for rape. We begged them to rape us, but they drove off into the night. I walked down to the highway every night for weeks after that, hoping to see them again.

Our debt-free home in Tulsa shortly before we moved to the wilderness in 1947

Remodeling back of farmhouse—finally blankets are gone. Tree on right is what is left after tornado hit. 1950

Our family in Central Park which adjoined Grandma and Gramps Calvert's front yard in Tulsa, Oklahoma 1946

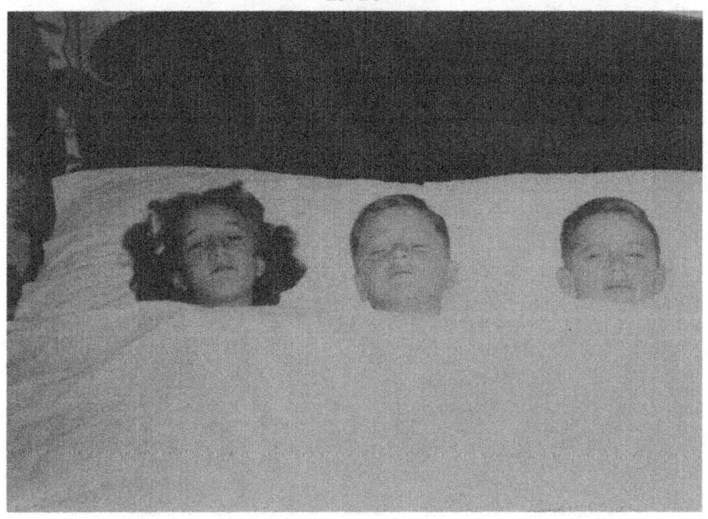

The night before Christmas, and all was well, except we're out of propane, and it's cold as hell. 1949

Tom wearing his new cowboy boots for the farm
Tulsa Rose Garden
1948

Dad and our new bathroom
1948

Grandma and Gramps Calvert on their
fiftieth wedding anniversary
1957

Visiting the Fulbrights, left to right: Sharon, a cousin,
Tom, Dad, Uncle Harry, and Grandpa Fulbright,
standing behind Dad, 1951

*Grandma and Grandpa Sherrill when they lived in
Jefferson, Texas
1953*

*Grandpa Sherrill getting a teeth-cleaning from his
pet parakeet at their home
1952*

Dad, Tom, and Gary cutting firewood
Winter 1948

Tom and Gary in small boat on our lake at the farm,
Laddy in the water
Summer 1947

The old barn on our farm
1947

Gary (in back) and a friend on Tom's horse Sugar
1948

PART TWO

A Dire Prediction

8

The Fever

Every spring my classmates and I liked to see who would be the first one to go swimming. Having no swimming pools, we used the nearest lake or pond. The year I was in the fifth grade, I figured it was my turn to be the earliest swimmer ever, so I announced my intention at school. All my classmates gathered together after school and we went as a large group to the chosen pond. No one else was willing to take the dare, so I jumped into the pond, which was still covered with a layer of ice, breaking through a hole into the icy cold water. After splashing around a few seconds in order to achieve my goal, I got out as quickly as I'd gotten in and became the big hero.

That night I started running a high fever. My temperature rose to 106 degrees and I went out of my head. When I tried to climb the walls, my parents took me to the hospital in Tulsa. Both my ears were infected, causing so much pressure to build, my eardrums burst. I lost about forty percent of my hearing. That was just the beginning. I then developed a strep infection, and without antibiotics, the infection turned in to rheumatic fever which affected my heart. This illness resulted in a heart murmur, an enlarged heart, and damaged heart valves. My parents came to see me every day for the week that I was in the hospital. After that I stayed with my grandparents until I was out of danger. I missed many weeks of school and my life never seemed quite the same after this illness.

I was finally allowed to go home after missing most of the school year. One night while lying in bed, I heard my parents talking to each other about me. "The doctor said that Tommy won't live to be thirty years old," my mother said.

"He probably lost a lot of his brain cells with that high fever," my father said.

I didn't realize this conversation would have the effect that it did. The next day my parents told me I should wait and take the fifth grade over, but I talked them out of that. It would have been terrible to be pushed back behind my friends, so they agreed to let me finish out the year with my class. I had made good grades up until I got sick, but I never truly caught up. I believed that what I'd heard my parents say was true. This gave me a reason to be a fun-loving kid with no brain cells the rest of my school days and to never worry about my grades. I don't know how I ever got through school. What difference did it make since I was going to die before I was thirty? I was thin and sickly looking, and all the doctors except one restricted me from any stress or physical activity.

Lucky for me, I had a heart specialist whose name you won't believe, but it's the honest truth. Dr. Safety First disagreed with the other doctors and started me on a body building program. (Why would anyone name their child Safety?) He encouraged me to be involved in all sports. Although I failed every physical during my high school and college years, Dr. First signed special forms giving me permission to play. He saved my life! Today I can pass any physical and I have no signs of heart disease, but my parents may have been right about the brain cells.

My relationship with my mother changed in some significant way after my illness, which may help to explain some of the changes in my behavior post-fifth grade. I think she believed the doctors prediction that I would die before I was thirty, so she let me get away with anything. I used this to my advantage. Before my illness my parents always knew they could depend on me. When work needed to be done, Gary would run off, but they knew they could get Tommy to do it, and they were right. If Dad said to mow the yard, it got done. After my illness, something began to change.

Our yard was not your normal yard. The portion of our land that Dad fenced off around our house was three acres, or about the size of a city block. We mowed this estate with a push mower, and it took two hard days to accomplish the task. Dad finally bought a riding mower and did it ever save time. One day as he was leaving for work, he said, "When I get home I want this place to look like a park." Gary had run off over the horizon, and I just got sick of it. I turned down the county road on the lawn mower. Before I knew it, I was on the main highway headed to town. I don't think Dad would have found me, but when I met a car I was forced to mow the right of way. When he came after me, he just followed the fresh cut grass.

I think after this my parents started to notice that it wasn't as important to me to please them. They started to worry about my lack of responsibility. The next week the new riding mower wouldn't start. Dad lifted the mower into the car, cussing every moment, and took it to the repair shop. I was glad because I had weekend plans to hitchhike to Tulsa with some friends to go swimming at a new city pool. The next morning Dad got up and said, "The mower has been fixed," and then the usual, "I want this place to look like a park before I get home."

I heard Gary crawling out the bedroom window and I saw him disappear across the prairie. I told Dad that I had plans to go swimming. That didn't matter; he still wanted the place to look like a park. I went outside and rolled the repaired mower out of the garage. I took the spark plug out and took a hammer and beat the end off. I quickly replaced it so Dad wouldn't notice. Then I told Dad I was having trouble starting the mower. "I'll start the damn thing before I leave for work," he said.

He came down ready for work dressed in a suit and tie. It was a hot, humid July day and by eight o'clock it was already in the high eighties. He grabbed the cord and jerked with all his might, and to his surprise nothing happened. I just stood there looking amazed. "Hmm," I said. He did this again and again, and now his coat was off and sweat was running off his head like a waterfall. I was starting to worry he might have a heart attack. Part of me wanted to tell him the truth, but I was afraid to. He must have pulled that cord a hundred times. I also heard some new cuss words. He was completely wet and red in the face and mad as hell. He grabbed the mower, threw it in the trunk of his car, and as he drove off, I heard him say he was going to cram the mower up some mechanic's ass. I headed to my friend's house and we hitchhiked to Tulsa and had a great day at the pool.

That night I was in trouble. The mechanic told Dad that someone had taken the spark plug out and probably smashed it with a hammer. Dad was furious and told my mother that I was turning into a delinquent. I heard Mother say, "It's probably because of the high temperature and his brain damage." This gave me a perfect out—I could always be brain dead.

Maybe it was the change I sensed in the relationship with my parents that affected the way I tried to attract friends. I discovered that in order to make friends, it helped to buy them. I had the perfect device: unlimited credit. My dad had opened a charge account for us at the local cafe and grocery store. My brother and sister had no problem with this; they used it only when necessary. On the other hand, I looked at it as a tool to win and influence friends.

Overnight I became the most popular kid in school. At lunch time or after school, I suggested to one or more of my classmates that they join me for lunch or an after-school snack. For over a month I was loved by all. Then one day all hell broke loose. Dad went by to pay his monthly bill. It was well over a hundred dollars and these were the days when a good job paid three hundred per month. Dad brought all the signed tickets home and almost all were mine. I didn't learn a lesson from this incident, however, because I still spent the next forty years trying to buy my friends.

Probably out of desperation, I decided to start a gang. I was a Cub Scout, and after our weekly Cub Scout meetings, I would meet my friends in the basement under our old farm house. It was the perfect hideout for a gang. Our first official task was deciding on a name. We liked the sound of "black studs," and since there were seven of us we called ourselves the Seven Black Studs. We needed money so we discussed ideas and voted on each one. Bob came up with the best suggestion: our gang would operate a protection racket. We signed up for a Post Office box and mailed a letter to all the merchants in town. Our letter was simple. It ordered each merchant to mail five dollars in cash to our P.O. box number or their business would be terrorized by the S.B.S.

We could hardly wait to go to the mail box the first of the month. We were amazed to find no money in the box. We held a special meeting of the S.B.S and voted to give the merchants a little scare. Our first victim would be the Pool Hall. That afternoon our little gang headed for the back of the Pool Hall. We picked up a concrete block and heaved it through the back door window. As we were running around the building, we ran into the only policeman in town. We were taken to City Hall, and since we were underage, our parents were called. Our town had an old fashioned City Council. The City Council didn't think it was fair for parents to pay damages or fines when their children had committed the crime. They made us kids work off the damages and fines by working on the streets or other city projects.

U.S. Highway 75 went through our town. Most of the cars traveling through were from out of state. Our first work assignment was to put up new speed limit signs. All Seven Black Studs were working on this project. While our supervisor went to get some ice water, I noticed a twenty-foot-long log chain in the back of the work truck. I had a great idea! We quickly grabbed the chain and tied it around our ankles. When a car approached us, we carried our picks and shovels on our shoulders and trudged along the highway like a chain gang—seven little kids chained together being forced to work in the hot Oklahoma sun. We would never have guessed the consequences.

Someone from out of state stopped at City Hall and threatened to call the governor. Someone else wrote a letter to our City Council complaining about the mistreatment of minors. Week after week the Tulsa newspaper received mail about child abuse and child labor laws. Needless to say, this worked in our favor. The mayor of our town got so angry that he let us all off. For a while a few reporters that didn't believe the story kept digging to find the truth.

As a result of our chain gang success, some of the members wanted to rob a blind man in a nearby town. He ran a shoe store, and while waiting on customers, he left his cash register unattended. Their plan was to go in and act like they were interested in shoes while the other gang members would take his money. This was when I began to lose control of the Seven Black Studs.

I have my grandmother to thank for this. One of the good things she taught me was to ask myself if what I was going to do would hurt or harm anyone. I used this throughout my life and it kept me out of some serious trouble.

Some of our gang members were not interested in the safety of others. We had always pulled tricks on people without hurting anyone, much less than to steal. My views were overruled, most of the members voting for it and calling the rest of us chickens. They headed out for the big robbery. After they stole the money, they made the mistake of showing off their cash at school. The police showed up and all of them were arrested. What they hadn't considered was the blind man was not completely blind, and he came to school and pointed out the guilty ones. The Black Studs were history.

Since my gang adventures had not worked out, I decided to become the most decorated Cub Scout in the history of scouting. Every page of a scouting manual has all kinds of projects and public service work. As a scout completed these projects, many of which were difficult, a parent was to check the work and sign that the scout had completed his project. The scout would then receive arrowheads to be sewn on his scout uniform. I wanted those arrowheads in the worst way.

I started working on every project in the book. They were too difficult and took too much time and effort. Then I discovered forgery. I could sign my mother's name better than she. Since my parents didn't have time to go to Cub Scout meetings and Dad never made it to the father-son dinners, I became the most decorated Cub Scout in a short period of time. I had arrowheads all over my uniform. In fact I didn't have room for all of them! My Cub Scout leader was impressed; she thought I was perfect.

Then one day I learned I had won the highest award a Cub Scout could win—the Webolow Award! I had never read what I was forging, so consequently I didn't know I had gone too far. When they called me up front to receive the award, the Master of Ceremonies said, "Tommy, how about reciting some of the Bible verses you memorized." It wasn't so bad being kicked out of the Cub Scouts, but they took all of my damn arrowheads.

I think it was about this same time that I first experimented with smoking. Bob came over and brought some grape vines to smoke. We really thought we were big shots sucking on these sticks. They were hard to light, but if we used kitchen matches, we could usually achieve the desired red glow as the sticks smouldered. I put a huge handful of matches in my pocket and forgot they were there. Later that day Bob and I went up on my parents' bed and were jumping up and down. The kitchen matches started rubbing together and ignited in my pants pocket. The fire burned a hole the size of a quarter in my leg.

Giving up on grape vines, I decided to smoke other things. I tried rolling up coffee grounds in a small piece of paper I tore out of my Big Chief tablet, but choked on the dry coffee when I sucked on my "cigarette." Next I rolled up notebook paper with nothing in it and lit the end of it. This time I sucked the flame down my throat. It was twenty more years before I smoked anything again.

Maybe experimenting with behavior that disappointed my parents made me braver—and that's a good thing. One time I was riding in the car with Dad when he was in a big rush to pick up Mother. He shot through a school zone going forty miles per hour. A policeman pulled him over, walked up to his window, and informed him that he was exceeding the speed limit. This was before radar, and the police guessed at your speed. Dad defended himself. "The hell I was! I was going twenty-five miles per hour." He had just convinced the policeman of his innocence when I remembered how nice that highway patrolman had been to me on Gary's scooter.

"Sir, just before you stopped us, I looked at the speedometer and we were going over forty," I said. As we drove off with our ticket, Dad told me there was a time to tell the truth and a time to lie, and if ever I was in doubt, lie.

It also took courage for me to ride the train to Tulsa all by myself. I learned that I could buy a round-trip ticket for only thirty-eight cents! My folks would give me one dollar to spend. The movie cost ten cents, and a coke and an all-day sucker cost a dime. The downtown theaters in Tulsa were like opera houses. Sometimes I think I was more interested in the beautiful theaters than the movie. One had stars and clouds on the ceiling and it was just like being outside lying on your back looking up at the sky. My mother told me that one movie was off limits, the Cozy, because it was on the wrong side of the tracks. This made me want to go see it more than anything, and I did. It was a mistake. A man sat down beside me and tried to touch me. I should have listened.

In the summertime a lot of people would go to the movies just to get out of the heat. The theaters would bring in huge blocks of ice and stack them in front of large fans. The air blowing over the ice would cool the whole building. After the movie I usually had enough money left for a couple of Coney's. Sometimes I would walk to Grandma's house to watch her panic because her little grandchild was all alone. She would walk me to the train station, make sure I got on the train, and send me home.

9

Prosperity

Owasso, the nearest small town, was located near a large aircraft maintenance center and a huge military contractor. The old farm and other land my parents had purchased were now in a prime location. After the war thousands of veterans were looking for some kind of affordable housing.

The veterans could use their government-issued guaranteed loans, but only on homes that didn't exceed a total payment of seventy-eight dollars per month, including principle, interest, taxes, and insurance. Most of the loans required payments of only sixty-eight dollars per month. The new F.H.A. and V.A. homes would be very simple. They would have approximately 850 square feet, one bathroom, three small bedrooms, no garage, no fireplace, no carpet, no air-conditioning, and no central heat. Most families in America at that time raised two or three kids in this type of housing.

My parents were interested in developing Owasso into a large suburb of Tulsa. It was their chance and their American dream to do this and make lots of money. It wasn't going to be easy. Owasso had no utilities, no good streets, and no sewer. It would be difficult to develop and sell new homes with outhouses. The first thing was to organize a Chamber of Commerce and then try to get a bond issue passed for a sewer system. The telephone system also needed to be updated. My parents worked seven days a week trying to bring about these changes with help from other interested merchants. The main obstacle they were unaware of was that a lot of people in that area didn't want progress and the growth that comes with it.

The first and second effort to pass the bond issue failed miserably, but with utmost determination, the third bond issue passed and opened up the way for development. The highway from Tulsa to Owasso was old and narrow and crossed several one-lane bridges. During the flood season, our small town was unreachable from Tulsa. My parents and others made many trips to the state capitol to try to get funds for a new highway and bridge. With the help of other investors, they were able to open the first new subdivision in Owasso since statehood. They had helped organize the first Chamber of Commerce and a new system of city government. A new telephone system was established and plans were underway for a new highway.

As my parents were getting better known in the community and making more money, they were able to finish the remodel on the old farm house. Everything we owned got better; even our cows had meat on their bones. Our fancy new house gave my parents a nice place to entertain—and they did it in grand style. Having plenty of liquor available for their guests was a strong indication of their prosperity, an image they wanted to convey.

During Oklahoma prohibition anyone could buy whiskey from the local bootlegger and have it delivered to his back door. Bootleggers were like doctors or lawyers—everyone had one. Our bootlegger owned a motel in Collinsville. Many times Dad would ask me to go up and ring the bell. It didn't matter how old you were. If you had the money, you got the booze.

In Tulsa there was a hot tamale salesman on the street corner. He had a cart with an umbrella and his stand was always open. We drove by many times and he was always busy. Years later I found out he was a bootlegger. Underneath his tray of hot steamy hot tamales was a large selection of liquor.

My dad hid most of his booze in the back of the kitchen cabinet or in the attic. He didn't fear the police or the federal agents—he only feared my Grandma. My friend Jimmy and I stole a gallon of Dad's gin and hid it inside an old mulberry tree. We knew we weren't old enough to drink, so we made a pact that in a few years we would come back to this orchard, get drunk, and talk about the old days. Coming home on the bus a couple of months later, I noticed that Dad was already home. He was out in the orchard trying to wake up some guy lying on the ground. Dad had hired Fred, the town drunk, to cut down some of our older mulberry trees. Fred must have thought he'd died and gone to heaven when the first tree he cut down concealed a gallon of gin.

Throughout my lifetime I have been exposed to countless tragedies brought on by people drinking. When we are young, we don't always see the dangers surrounding alcohol. I have known many fun-loving people who now hide their tears behind a bottle of beer. When I watch television ads with beautiful high-spirited people in bars, we should also see ads depicting the tragedies of drinking—broken families, violence, adultery, and injury or fatalities resulting from drunk driving.

As my parents were making more money, they were able to hire help in the house and on the farm. One day they arrived home with an African American couple. The woman looked a lot like Aunt Jemima on the syrup bottle. Her husband was tall and weathered-looking. My mother introduced the new workers as James and Bessy. Bessy would keep the house and do the washing, and James would help on the farm. I stayed away from these strangers for some time, just watching them do their work and never talking unless I was spoken to. Mother would have killed us if we had said anything disrespectful. The first thing I noticed was that black people talked differently when white people were not around. Often I hid and listened to them talking when they thought no one was home. I also discovered they had feelings and cared about their families. It took me awhile, but I finally realized that James and Bessy were just like me, only black.

James was seventy-nine when he started working on our farm. As a young man, he worked on ranches in Texas and Oklahoma. He could rope and ride better than anyone I had ever seen. His job on these ranches was to break wild horses. He was even able to catch our horses! Bessy was probably a little younger, but she didn't think it was any of our business how old she was. She was very polite, never showed any anger, and I felt that she cared about me. She worried that I didn't have proper supervision. I asked her lots of questions about being black and how she felt about that. Her response would always be the same: "That's just the way it is."

James and Bessy had a grandson named Larry who lived in Chicago. He got into some kind of trouble, so his parents sent him to live with his grandparents. Bessie thought Larry and I had a lot in common; neither of us had enough supervision. Larry was the nicest kid I had ever met. He loved helping on our farm and was pleasant to have around. It hurt me when people would call these good black people "niggers" and make fun of them. I could see the hurt in their eyes. James, Bessie, and Larry became a part of our family. Larry hung around with me some, but I could see that he wasn't like the black kids in Oklahoma. He didn't go for the "Uncle Tom" act and rebelled against the Oklahoma segregation rules. This caused him some problems in Tulsa, but not in our small town of Owasso.

Years later when Larry was getting older, my mother became concerned about his future education. She talked to Bessy and James and told them she would set up a scholarship fund for Larry if he graduated with good scores. He made good grades and graduated, but he also started running around with some black militant friends. He told my mother he wasn't about to take any of "Whitey's" money. To this day I don't know what happened to him.

My Grandma Sherrill from Texas came to spend the summer one year when James and Bessy were working for us. (What a horrible thought—three months with more supervision!) I knew there would be trouble when she arrived. Dad had not told his mother that a black maid worked in our house and a black man worked on our farm. She treated them like dirt, but they just did their jobs and didn't say a word. After a few weeks of hell, we were all sitting at the dinner table on Sunday when Grandma Sherrill made a bad mistake. "Either these niggers leave or I'm going back to Texas," she said.

"Then I think it's time for you to go back to Texas," my mother said. Grandma left and never came back to our home in Oklahoma.

After ten years had gone by, Dad no longer needed the extra help. Bessy and James, both in their late-eighties, were just about worn out. I asked Dad, "What are you going to do about a retirement for them?" Dad answered, "What the hell are you talking about? I'm going to sell them!" For a few years I stopped by their house on a small acreage in north Tulsa to keep in touch, but one day they were no longer there. I learned they had both died.

With newfound prosperity, our family was one of the first families in Oklahoma to own a speedboat. The boat dealer delivered our new Larson boat with a big twenty-five horse power Evinrude motor. We were all excited to get to Fort Gibson Lake and try it out. It was late Friday night and already dark before we arrived, but when we got there, the boat dealer had our beautiful boat already in the water and ready to go. The salesman gave Dad four or five minutes of instructions and turned us loose. Dad started up the powerful rumbling motor, and we slowly left the dock and headed out onto the dark lake. The only light we could see was from a few cabins on the shore. Gradually Dad picked up speed. Before we knew it, our fourteen-foot boat was running at full speed, skimming along the lake's surface, smooth as glass. Over and over Dad went straight for the lights on shore, and just before running into the bank, he turned sharply to save us. We would all laugh and scream. We zipped around the big lake back and forth at least an hour before Dad finally decided that was enough for one night. He had rented a little cabin on the lake, and we all had trouble going to sleep that night we were so excited with anticipation for the morning to come.

I woke up at daylight and ran out of our small cabin and headed to the shore to look at the lake we had so bravely traversed the night before. What a shock! That lovely lake was a river full of tree stumps and sand bars! I ran back to the cabin and woke everyone up. They jumped out of bed and ran with me to the shore. No one could believe we hadn't hit a tree or run aground the night before. It was a miracle.

After gathering up our nerve to go back out with Dad, we filled up both tanks with gas and, with map in hand, headed up river in the boat to the main part of the lake. Only a few small fishing boats were out, and we waved hello to all of them. Everyone wanted to stop and talk to us about our new speedboat. Dad also loved to race any boat we ran into that had the same size motor. When we stopped at the fishing village to get more gas, everyone there raved about our beautiful boat. It was 1952 and we felt like millionaires!

As the day progressed, Dad drove us further and further from our dock and cabin. The river we started out on was now a large lake with fifteen hundred miles of shore line. Even a person who had been on this lake for years could get lost. It was still daylight and Dad said we had better head back. Well, it was too late; we were about twenty-five miles from our dock and there were forks heading in every direction.

As we frantically searched our map for the right way to go, our worst fear came true. The sun went down and when the sun goes down on the lake, the lake gets very dark. Our little family was now out in the middle of a huge lake with no idea where we were. Since we had narrowly escaped disaster on our first night out, Dad drove our small craft extremely slow in the dark. He was only able to see a few feet ahead and, with no visible lights on the shore, we slowly and very quietly headed north. Frequently Dad broke the silence by saying, "I think this is the way." He didn't have a clue about where he was, and we knew it. Soon we saw water reeds sticking up out of the water, and eventually trees. Then a fog set in and our motor hit bottom, killing the engine. It was so quiet you could hear fish jump and an occasional frog croak. We must have sat there in the idle boat for ten minutes in silence, when all of a sudden Mother jumped up and screamed as loud as she could, "We're going to die!" Well, this was really smart. Sharon started to cry, Dad and Mother got in a fight, and Gary and I were scared to death. We were all yelling or screaming at once. I guess this was real panic.

Finally I said, "What's going to kill us?" Everyone fell silent and then suddenly we all started laughing. We slept all night in our speedboat. In the light of dawn, we managed to get out of the mud and find our way back to our dock. Everyone there had been worrying about us, but Dad tried to act like we camped out on purpose. This was Mother's first and last trip to the lake.

Weeks later I learned to drive the boat and I was dying to show off my new skill. I wasn't old enough to drive the car so I couldn't pull the boat to the lake to show my friends. Instead I invited all my friends to our farm and we pulled the boat on its trailer to our pond. We launched it and started it up, but we could only go in small circles. It was still fun. Some neighbor must have seen us and told Dad, so that was the end of that.

Dad sold farms and ranches to many people from New York. These buyers who came out to Oklahoma were usually rich and looking for a place to invest their money. Ranches were a good tax shelter in the fifties, and Oklahoma had plenty of land. Most of the people from up north had never been this far west, and they expected to see buffalo and Indians running wild.

One night my parents were having an outdoor dinner party for some of these New York city slickers. I thought it would be fun to provide some entertainment. My friend Ronnie's greatest attribute was an amazing ability to imitate just about any animal. Once he got us all fired from a job we had at the Tulsa Zoo by barking like a hyena. It sounded so real, you wouldn't believe it! All the zoo animals went crazy. The zoo superintendent told us never to come back, even as paying customers!

Ronnie and two other friends and I snuck out to the pasture and slowly worked our way toward the house in the dark. When we got within ear shot, Ronnie began to make coyote and wolf noises, keeping this up until we heard some of the guests expressing concern about their safety. Dad reassured them that they were safe, but that only encouraged Ronnie to howl louder. The next thing we knew Dad ran out the back door with a shotgun and fired into the air four or five times. The coyotes and wolves ran for cover as quickly as two legs could carry them.

In time Dad and Mom subdivided some of our own farm into twenty-five-acre parcels for nice country homes. Our first new neighbor was Bill, a tall 250 pound man. His wife was a beautiful, Osage Native American woman loaded with money. Bill's friends were all a bunch of fun-loving drunks. Bill called me one day and asked me if I wanted to make some money by helping him lay sod on his new estate. I agreed and we worked for about an hour until some of his friends came by and took him to the local bar. Before he left he gave me twenty dollars and said, "Tom, is this enough for today?"

I thought I'd discovered a gold mine when he called me again the next day wanting to know if I was ready to work some more. "You bet!" I said. We worked hard side by side until it was so dark we could hardly see. When we finished up, he reached in his pocket to pay me. I was expecting one hundred dollars or more, but he handed me a five dollar bill and said, "Thanks."

Bill would let me drive his new "Caddy" around his estate as long as I didn't take it out on the road since I was only thirteen years old. While some of his friends were there one day, he asked me to take his car up to the bootlegger in Collinsville and get a couple of bottles. He called ahead and gave me the money. I was in hog heaven driving on the back roads for the first time in a brand new 1955 Cadillac! When I got to Collinsville, I had to drive two blocks on the main U.S. Highway. I picked up the booze and headed back. Bill was very proud of me and advised me not to tell my parents. I agreed.

After that I would "accidentally" drop by every time I saw Bill's friends at his house. He usually would want me to do something, or I just got a good laugh listening to these guys. One day they sent me to town to pick up a bag of ice. I drove right down Main Street in Bill's new Cad. I was just tall enough to look between the horn and the top of the steering wheel. I drove right by my parents' office and saw Dad look out, do a double-take, and then shake his head. He never knew it was me!

Bill's friends brought him a large, and I do mean large, black Doberman Pincer. Bill named the dog Chris, and it was so vicious even Bill had a hard time controlling him. Chris hated me and tried to bite me every chance he got. One Sunday morning I went out to get the paper. I was wearing only my underwear. As I reached down to get the paper, I saw Chris out of the corner of my eye. Our house was about fifty yards from the road and Chris was about the same distance from me. Hoping to outrun Chris to the house, I took off at full speed to reach the front door, falling into the entryway. I had made it, but I no longer had on my undershorts; Chris had them in his mouth.

If I was going over to Bill's house, I had to call first or take a chance on being attacked by his dog. Bill finally built a six foot chain link fence around his twenty-five-acre yard and he had an electric gate installed. He didn't work except in his yard and it was his pride and joy. One afternoon I was visiting Bill. His wife was looking for her pet Chihuahua that wasn't much bigger than a rat. I looked over in the corner where Chris was lying and I could see the Chihuahua's tail sticking out of Chris's mouth. Bill pried Chris's mouth open and got the wet but unharmed Chihuahua out.

Another day I was sitting in a chair in Bill's den and, to my surprise, Chris walked over and laid his head in my lap. Very cautiously I gently petted this vicious dog, and he seemed to enjoy this. Bill walked into the room and, with panic in his voice, said, "Whatever you do, don't stop petting him or he will bite you—but if you pet him too long he will bite you too."

10

Employment

Looking back on my own growing up, I realize I had other people in my life besides my parents who taught me some important lessons about responsibility and hard work. It's hard to say which individuals helped me most, the positive or the negative role models. A case in point is the family of one of my closest friends Jack. Jack's parents owned a large dairy farm. His dad was the town drunk, and due to a long illness, he was unable to work on the farm. Jack's mother began teaching at the age of sixteen and taught in the public school system for over fifty years. She also was active in her church and cared for many people in the community. For all the years she worked in Owasso, she was an important influence on many children, including me.

Mrs. Richardson, Jack's mother, was my first grade teacher. She told a story about me in the first grade that I had tried to forget. Learning to recognize our own printed names was one of our earliest lessons. On her desk was a small imitation tree from which hung ten pieces of candy taped to ten small cards with each student's name printed on one of them. As we came in each morning, if we could correctly identify our own name, we could take the piece of candy off the tree. I had not yet been able to do this. She reminded me of the day I came in when only one name remained. I smiled big, pointed to my name, and finally got to pluck off my candy.

That same year we made an art project in class. One day in her home some thirty years later, I noticed the ugliest looking napkin holder I had ever seen. I asked her where she got the ugly thing and she told me to turn it over and read the name on the bottom. Expecting to make fun of my friend Jack, I was amazed to discover that it had been me who had made the ugly napkin holder. She was a special teacher.

Unfortunately Jack's dad was the meanest and surliest man in town. Jack and his mother milked all the cows on their farm at four in the morning and five-thirty at night, seven days a week. His dad called Jack's mother names so bad I dare not repeat them in this book. Many times he did this in front of me as well as Jack's other friends. The strange thing was, even with all of his faults, almost everyone in town liked him. He was known as Uncle Cys (pronounced "cease"). Like many drunks, he did many colorful and funny things. He got lots of laughs, but at the same time he was heartbreak to his family.

Uncle Cys had asthma so bad he couldn't lie down at night to sleep. Consequently he slept standing up with his head resting on his folded arms every night, all night, in this position. During the day, he would sit in the kitchen where he was able to see out the window to keep a watch over his farm. He also watched every move Jack and I made. After school when I went over to help Jack milk cows, I was always greeted with, "Hello, you dumb son-of-a-bitch," or "What are you dumb sons-of-bitches up to?" This was his favorite expression.

One day I stumbled across an article about a cure for asthma. It maintained that if a small dog like a Chihuahua was kept near the asthma sufferer at all times, it would eventually cure the illness. I told Uncle Cys about what I had read, and he told me he was willing to try any remedy. Having to sleep in an upright position was a problem, and without the asthma, he would be able to work on his farm.

Jack and I took off for Tulsa and bought a Chihuahua. We brought home the smallest, skinniest dog I had ever seen and gave it to Uncle Cys. He kept this dog on the kitchen cabinet next to him at all times. After a few months of living on the counter, the skinny dog looked like it had been blown up with an air pump, but instead of curing Uncle Cys of his ailment, the dog now had asthma too. Both Uncle Cys and his dog fought for air.

One afternoon Uncle Cys called Jack and me into the kitchen. He was concerned about his fence by the main road which crossed the creek. He wanted our help in building a new fence with a swing gate. This was no small task and Jack and I were pleased he trusted us to help with this important job. A swing gate across a creek has to keep cattle in during normal times. During a flood, however, when the creek is full of logs and trash, the swing gate should swing up and let the trash pass through. When the water recedes, the swing gate should then fall back down while hanging on a large cable that supports the fence. Uncle Cys was not able to do any work, but he wanted to locate the best place for us to build a new fence. He and his Chihuahua got into his work truck and they drove to the job site to pick a spot for the fence. The place he decided on was excellent. On one side of the creek was a huge tree which would support one end of the cable. The other side would need a large steel post cemented into the ground in order to be as strong as the tree on the other side.

When Uncle Cys went back to his kitchen spot to watch us carry tools back and forth to the work area, it was almost a comfort to look back and see his lips moving. We laughed because we knew he was saying, "You dumb sons-of-bitches!" When we finally had all the tools in place, we tied the cable to the strong tree on the west side of the creek and stretched it across to the other side. After digging a hole only four or five inches deep, we hit solid rock and our troubles began. After hours of chipping away with picks, we gave up and went to town and borrowed an air compressor and a drill. All we had to say was, "Uncle Cys" and people loaned us anything.

We needed to drill a six-inch wide hole large enough to hold a six-inch diameter steel pipe and concrete around it. The air compressor and drill worked a little better than the picks, but we still were not getting the results we needed to get the fence up. Then it hit us—DYNAMITE! In the fifties, a person could buy dynamite from the local feed store. No federal rules or regulations existed. Many farmers used dynamite to blow tree stumps and rocks out of their fields. We took off to town again where we asked the feed store owner for advice as to what we needed. He recommended two sticks of dynamite, and we could come back for more if that wasn't enough. Our project was getting exciting.

We decided to take eight sticks, and we told the feed store man that we'd bring back any leftovers. On our way back to the farm, we stopped and picked up an old man who lived in the local bars. He had told us numerous times that he had worked on the Hoover Dam as a dynamite expert. After a run to the store for a couple of six packs for him, we were ready to blow up rocks.

When we arrived at the fence site, Uncle Cys and a group of his friends had arrived in pickup trucks to watch. Uncle Cys was hanging out of his truck window waving a whiskey bottle in the air. "All you dumb sons-of-bitches come over here for a drink," he yelled. As Jack and I worked on drilling a six-foot deep hole with the air compressor, the spectators finished off the bottle of whiskey with Uncle Cys.

The dynamite expert told us to use four sticks at once since the rock was solid. He described a special way to place the sticks so when they went off they would blow down into the rock and not up. He personally guaranteed not one rock would jump off the ground over six inches. We believed he knew what he was doing. Jack and I carefully attached the caps and electric wire to each stick of dynamite and, one by one, we dropped each one down into the narrow hole, using a wood pole to tamp each stick down like loading a cannon.

Just when we thought we could start the show, Uncle Cys pointed out a telephone cable above our blast site which carried hundreds of telephone lines in the area. He was a little worried about a rock flying up and severing the cable, putting telephone lines out of service. The dynamite man resented his authority being questioned and was about to head back to the bar. Uncle Cys quickly announced that there would be food and drinks for all the helpers after the job was done, so the expert stayed.

Jack suggested we get the twelve-gallon steel milk cooler from their dairy barn to place over the blast site in case a few rocks flew up unexpectedly. Everyone agreed this was a good idea, so we went after the cooler and drug it down a gravel road behind a tractor. It must have weighed as much as a car.

When everything was finally in place, the expert took the wire and batteries and went under the bridge to hide behind a concrete pier. (This in itself should have told us something.) The rest of us backed up about thirty feet and stood by Uncle Cys's truck. "Fire in the hole!" the dynamite man hollered. A low rumble erupted from the earth and for a short moment our feet trembled, but nothing could have prepared us for the explosion that followed. The two-ton milk cooler shot straight up in the air like a rocket ship, and on its way up, it took the phone cable with it. Thousands of rocks, some as big as school desks, blew up into the air; rubble and debris were flying everywhere. Jack, Uncle Cys, all his friends, and I took off running for our lives. As I looked back, the scene resembled an airplane explosion. I also saw Uncle Cys backing up his truck at full speed—he had the right idea.

When all the rocks, dirt, cooler parts, and cable pieces finally came to a rest, a huge hole big enough for a house was left in the ground. The bridge on the main road was covered with two or three feet of dirt and rock. Word quickly traveled about the explosion and people came from miles to see the gaping hole. We were extremely lucky that no one was hurt.

It took us hours to get the bridge cleaned off so cars could cross. The telephone company spent days restoring service to their customers. We used thirteen yards of concrete and loads of rocks and dirt to fix the steel post in the ground. I went by this swing gate and steel post thirty-five years later and it was still there.

Summers in Oklahoma were so hot even the ponds we swam in were like taking a hot bath. In this heat one of the hardest jobs in the world was hauling hay, but it was the only job that Gary, I, or my friends could always get in the summer. If we were too young to throw hay on the wagon or truck, we could still get a job driving a truck. The farmer told us to put the truck in low gear, or "put it in granny," and then all you had to do was ride and steer it between the endless rows of hay. We made fifty cents a ton which was equivalent to thirty bales of hay, and these had to be loaded on a truck, taken to the barn, unloaded, and stacked neatly in the shed. It was grueling work for fifty cents a ton. On a good day we hauled ten tons and made five dollars. We worked all week.

Our favorite thing to do on payday was to get dressed up and get a ride or take the train to Tulsa and go directly downtown to Bishop's Restaurant. It was the best and most expensive place in town. A steak cost five dollars with all the trimmings, or as we said, a steak cost ten tons of hay. Everything we did was based on how many tons of hay we had to move. By the end of the weekend we were always broke.

Later in our high school years, we took dates to Tulsa and spent twenty tons or ten dollars for dinner. Everyone liked to spend their hay money in different ways. One of our friends spent fifty to sixty tons or thirty dollars at the May Rooms, a low-class whorehouse. After dinner we stopped by there to pick up our broke friend.

I don't know how it happened, but one day I woke up and knew it was time to get a good job. Coincidentally Bob came over that same week and said, "Hey Tom, the town of Owasso is looking for a dog catcher." The next morning we went down to town hall and applied. It was lucky for us the town had a new mayor who had no knowledge of the famous chain gang incident. He offered us one dollar for each dog we delivered to the pound. We accepted the offer. Bob was the Dog Catcher and I was his assistant.

Owasso furnished us with a city truck and all the nets and ropes we needed to do the job. Since the town had more stray dogs than people, we started out really well. Working as a team, we picked up about twenty dogs a day. Twenty dollars was good money for an easy job with a great title. One large Collie dog had a special bounty of five dollars. His bounty was higher because he was extremely mean and no catcher had been able to bring him in. One day Bob and I saw the Collie go under a house with no way out. Bob grabbed a rope and crawled under after him. He ended up fighting the dog on his hands and knees under the house. The noise from outside was horrible and when Bob finally emerged, he had dog bites on his face and arms. We never got that five dollar dog.

Eventually the dog business dried up. Because we did our job so well, no dogs were left to catch. Bob and I had grown accustomed to our new wages, so we knew we had to come up with a new idea. Bob suggested we take dogs out of their owners' yards and turn them in immediately in order to collect our bounty money. This worked for a short time until the townspeople began to complain. Then I suggested that we sneak down to the dog pound and let some of the dogs out, so in the morning there would be stray dogs in town. After catching and collecting our bounty, we could let them loose again on another night. We were soon fired and Bob and I were looking for another job.

11

About Town in the Fifties

Nationwide publicity came to our community in a way nobody could have predicted. The coverage centered around Don Davis, an Owasso man who owned the funeral home and a Coonhound named Little Richard. Coon hunters set up campfires along the Verdigris River and listened to their dogs work the woods and high bluffs along the river. If a dog spotted a coon, he would start barking, signaling to his owner-hunter that a chase was to begin. The hunter would follow the dog through the woods in the dark until the dog treed the coon, never knowing how far this chase could take him.

One night as Don and his friends sat by the campfire listening to Little Richard work the woods, the dog found a scent and took off after a coon. This coon was smarter than the average and ran into a cave instead of up a tree. The cave was part of a series of caves above the Verdigris River which ran back into the bluffs for hundreds of feet. Little Richard was hot on the coon's trail, but as the cave got smaller and smaller, the coon was able to escape down a long narrow passageway. Little Richard fell into a six-inch crevice and got stuck.

In anguish he bellowed for his owner. Don went into the cave as far as he could, crawling on his stomach in the mud. Unable to go any further and exhausted from the chase, he backed out, though he was still worried about his dog. He knew Little Richard was alive, but he also knew the dog wouldn't make it out of the cave without help.

The next day my friends and I learned about the plight of Little Richard and went to the caves offering to help. My friend Dillard, the smallest of our group, was able to crawl into the opening far enough to see and touch Little Richard's nose. After some effort we got food and water to the dog, which was the best we could do for the time. Our rescue mission quickly turned into an endurance test for Little Richard and someone told the newspaper about the trapped dog. This changed everything. People came from everywhere to see the dog, each with an idea about how to rescue Little Richard. When the Tulsa radio and television stations reported the story, my friends and I became less interested in the dog, and more interested in PUBLICITY!

Then the Associated Press picked up the story and camera crews began to arrive, along with emergency lights and generators. The American Red Cross was even there with food and medical aid. I must have eaten at least fifty sandwiches and drunk all the pop my stomach could hold. It was amazing having all these journalists in town and we tried to get as much attention as we could. The only problem for me was that Dillard had carried one of the cameras back into the cave to get a shot of Little Richard, so he was in the spotlight. I faked a fall off of a high bluff right in front of the reporters and even that didn't get me noticed.

Meanwhile the rescue continued. A large oil company took in a drilling rig, but soon realized that the solid rock was going to take too long to penetrate, and the dog was losing strength as each minute went by. Just as all hope was lost, a dynamite man from Nevada showed up. He had worked on building dams and had seen the reports on television about the hopeless situation of Little Richard. He asked me if I would help him carry his bags. While I walked along beside him, I told him about the incident on Jack's farm. He didn't know our town's dynamite expert and the nice thing about him was that he didn't seem to be drunk. I helped him set charges and gave pillows to Dillard to put near the dogs face. The man knew how to set charges and little by little he blasted his way toward Little Richard.

When at last the dog was freed, the workers celebrated and everyone wanted to touch the dog and help put him in the police car. With sirens blaring, the town police, the dog's owner, and Little Richard set off for town. All the crews followed as if we had saved the life of the President. Most of the people didn't hear about the end of this story. The next day Little Richard escaped from his kennel and was hit and killed by a car.

Every summer in Owasso, a group of migrating people we called the Gypsies set up camp just outside our town. Their camp site was always in the same place and consisted of old trailer houses and tents. Someone from town would spot them as they arrived and run up and down the street warning everyone that the Gypsies were in town. Gypsies were supposed to be the worst people in the world. It was told they would steal anything not tied down, so we were warned to hide our valuables and make sure our daughters were kept inside. During the day the Gypsies worked in town buying and selling goods, and then at nightfall, they would return to their camp. Their colorful head bands and strange accent aroused our curiosity, so my friends and I went out to their camp site to visit after dark. Their music and dancing was different from anything we had ever seen or heard. Now, when I hear Cajun music, it reminds me of our Gypsies. We had our fortunes told and listened to some great stories around their camp fires. Some local men from town were there talking to the young Gypsy women—the same men who had warned us of the dangers ascribed to these people. The Gypsies usually stayed for about one week before moving on, but one day in the mid-fifties, they disappeared forever.

Other strange people showed up around our area. One was a man everyone called Zeke. No one knew him or his last name, but he was a weekly sight walking the highways. Heading home on the school bus, our bus driver sometimes picked him up. Zeke was an older man with no money, and he wrapped his feet with feed sacks for shoes. He walked from Tulsa to Coffeyville, Kansas, picking up pop bottles along the way. He usually rode our bus for a few minutes (maybe to get warm) until he got nervous, and then he wanted off. Zeke walked as fast as anyone I have ever seen. He was always in a rush to get to the next pop bottle and to the next town to sell them. Sometimes we saw him in a cafe and he was a sad sight. He sat at the counter, always alone, dressed in dirty, torn, shabby clothes. Dad always bought his dinner if the owner wouldn't tell who had paid his bill. Zeke walked the two-hundred-mile round trip to Coffeyville and back most of my childhood, and then like so many other things in my life, he disappeared.

One time when we were driving home from Arkansas, we stopped at a small restaurant to eat. An obviously poor family came in while we were there and asked the owner if they could sing for their supper. He agreed and they stood there singing and playing musical instruments. Their music was good but they showed no emotion. There seemed to be so many families with nothing and on the edge of giving up. A lot of those faces I don't think I will ever forget.

Owasso had some very scary characters in town. I suppose every small town has its bully, but Owasso had four: the Braxton brothers. Each one was about five foot eight inches tall with legs only twenty-four inches long. They ran like a pack of wild bulldogs from town to town looking for someone to beat half to death. They terrorized the people in every bar and cafe in whatever town they were in, and they were usually good for a parking lot fight before they jumped into their car and took off to the next town. If they weren't beating a guy up, they shot or stabbed someone. Monday morning they all went to work as if nothing had happened, worked hard all week, and saved their money to go back out and do the same thing all over again.

The Braxtons avoided only one man in town and that was Claude. Claude was six-feet two-inches tall and weighed about 280 pounds. He would take on any comers, and I don't think Claude ever lost a fight. He also ran around with my neighbor Bill, and the two of them together were an awesome sight. Bill had the longest reach I had ever seen. He could place his fingertips on the edge of an eight-foot pool table and reach the other end. If anyone ever crossed Claude or Bill, they just picked the perpetrator up and threw him out into the street. One day during a shuffle board game, Bill got mad and took out his gun and shot the lights out in the bar. The owner kicked him out and locked the door. Bill was so mad, he got in his Cadillac, backed up across the parking lot, and then gunned the car forward into the side of the building, knocking down the concrete wall of the bar.

I liked Bill and Claude, probably because they paid a lot of attention to me. Anytime I ran into them I tried to think of something to make them mad. They seemed to enjoy chasing me, and roughing me up a little. One time I saw Bill's Caddy sitting in the parking lot of a bar in town. I went inside and sneaked up behind Bill and hit him as hard as I could in the back before running for the door. With the worst of luck, I ran into Claude who grabbed me and put me into a headlock. Then Bill grabbed my leg and one arm and Claude grabbed the opposite arm and leg and they threw me back and forth on the shuffle board table. These big, burly men were unlike my father, who was more of a pacifist, but I remember wanting to be like them.

The bars and pool halls of Owasso were the best places for us kids to meet lively characters. Every social misfit in town hung out at the pool hall. It was supposedly off-limits to kids, but it was also the first place parents went to look for their missing children. We loved the pool hall because we could act any way we wanted. The pool hall owner didn't tell on us because he was afraid the parents might get together and have the place shut down. The owner really didn't care if we spit on the floors, talked dirty, or got in fights. We loved to hide the pool balls to drive him crazy, and we won money on the pinball machines. The best pinball player was a kid named Johnny. He cheated a little by putting the front legs of the machine on top of his shoes to slow the ball down. This also made it easier to win. He became known as Pinball Johnny, and when he had marks on his shoes, we all knew he'd been at the pool hall. We also loved the juke box and our favorite song was "The Happy Organ."

One day the pool hall owner got sick of our mischief and took out his forty-five revolver to run us all out. An old man named One Arm Roy, a pool hall regular, took the gun away from the owner. Roy had traveled the world making his living on his wit. Although he was a great pool player, his best game was poker. He ran a game in the pool hall with a couple of the locals. Just being around them and listening to their stories made a trip to the pool hall fun.

A local bootlegger ran another bar in town. He had a bulldog so fat his stomach drug on the floor as he walked across the bar. The dog was famous for being particular about his beer. Different kinds of beer were poured into bowls for the dog. The dog would walk slowly down the line of bowls, stopping to drink only at the bowl containing Falstaff.

12

Risky Business

By the time I was fourteen, Gary began to show more interest in doing things with me. By then I was tough, very strong, and had no fear. After all, I was running out of time. Sometimes at night I helped him push our parents' car out of the driveway and down the road. When we were a safe distance from the house, we started the car and took turns driving on the back roads. We did this for many nights and were never caught by our parents. Just before we got close to our house on our way home, we would kill the engine and push the car back into the same spot on the drive.

I sensed that Gary needed me. He asked me to ride the rails with him. Together we walked to the railroad tracks and climbed into a box car and rode until the train stopped. Then we hitchhiked home. This was dangerous because we ran the risk of being injured or assaulted by some hobo. We also risked getting locked in a box car and left for days on a deserted siding while hiding from a railroad guard.

Ready for more action, I invited my friend Jim to hop a freight train with me to Kansas. We rode for several hours toward Coffeyville when the train stopped. Thinking we were there, we jumped off and there wasn't a soul in sight. We walked along a narrow two-lane road heading south and nobody picked us up. Finally two men stopped and asked us where we were going. "Tulsa, and we're in a hurry to get there," we said.

"Get in the car," the driver said. We were so relieved to get a ride because it was getting close to dark and we were worried. Just as we began to settle in for our return home, the two men turned off the main highway onto a dirt road and headed west. When Jim and I protested, the man in the passenger seat pulled out a gun, pulled the hammer back, and pointed it into our faces. "Do what we tell you or you're dead," he said.

They drove for a few miles to the end of a dirt road and told us to get out. I figured this was going to be the end of my life, and for some reason, I wasn't scared. Jimmy and I stood in the ditch on the side of the road waiting to be shot. The man pointed the gun at us and pulled the trigger. It was empty and they drove off laughing! Our troubles were not over though; we still had to make it back to the main highway. Every time we saw the lights of a car or a truck we hid. After a few hours we made it to the main highway and were finally able to get a ride home. The next day we learned that no one in our families even realized we'd been gone!

One Saturday night a big party was going on at the V.F.W. Hall in Collinsville. I really wanted to go, but everyone was older and had cars to drive. Dad had just bought a brand new 1956 Dodge convertible with power steering and push button drive. It was beautiful—bright purple with pure white leather seats.

Late that night I pushed our new car out of the drive. Since I couldn't push it very far, I had to start it close to the house. It started right up and I headed to the dance.

I told everyone that my dad had bought me this car for my sixteenth birthday. I was the hit of the party. Dragging Main Street with girls riding like beauty queens sitting on the top of the back seat, I felt like a real stud. Everyone wanted to be my friend. A little after midnight, I was dancing with this girl and feeling great, when I heard this loud voice. "Tommy, where the hell is my car!" It was my dad standing at the entrance to the V.F.W. Hall. Boy, was I embarrassed! Not only did Dad tell everyone out loud that it was not my car, he even said I was only fourteen years old and didn't have a drivers' license. I hadn't felt this bad since the day I lost all my arrowheads.

I remember spending a lot of time with my friends sitting in the local cafe trying to come up with some kind of fun or crazy idea to make life more interesting. I have wondered if it isn't this kind of boredom and lack of structure and support that propels kids today toward drugs. Our generation can be grateful that those temptations didn't abound during our adolescence. We thought only black people used drugs, so drugs weren't cool.

One of our most elaborate schemes to create excitement was concocted one afternoon when I was sipping cokes and eating moon pies with my friends Neil and Charlie. Just a few days before, I had read in the paper about a mysterious light in the sky that had alarmed thousands of people in and around Tulsa. The strange light turned out to be a prank pulled off by a bunch of kids from a Tulsa high school. They were arrested and charged with a misdemeanor for disturbing the peace. Then it hit me! We could create a monster story and become famous; the key would be to use mass hysteria. Our first step was to get a commitment from each other to swear never to reveal our prank to anyone. Then we got down to the details of our plan.

Our monster would be over seven-feet tall with a deformed face and a large hunched back. Neil and I would wear the monster outfit by Neil straddling my back. At that height and with Neil's looks, we didn't need much more intimidation. We also selected a dirt road with a one-lane bridge that wound through the river bottom to be the place for a sighting. Next we set the mood in town by telling stories about seeing a large hunched back figure at different times and places, hoping this would get the story circulating.

In only a few weeks, several people in town told me that they also had spotted a monster. The plan was working better than I had predicted; it was time for a real sighting. On the prescribed night, Charlie ran into the cafe shouting that he had just seen a huge man chasing a little guy down the road by the river. Charlie was a good actor and he also had his own car. He had everyone convinced that he had really seen a monster on that river road. Everyone except Neil and me, that is. At just the right moment, Neil jumped up and called Charlie a liar in front of everyone, triggering a convincing fist fight between them. To get even with Neil and to prove his credibility, Charlie offered to take some of the guys and girls from town out to look for the hunched back monster themselves. He had no trouble getting takers. As soon as Charlie and his unsuspecting group left the cafe, Neil and I ran out the back door and jumped on Gary's motor scooter, which we had stashed in the weeds for a quick getaway. Since it was imperative that we reach the bridge before Charlie and the onlookers, we took a short cut while Charlie took the long way to the bridge.

Neil and I took our positions on a knoll that would be in full view of the car when Charlie came over the bridge. I had ketchup on my face and Neil was on top of me prepared to act as though he was striking me with a rock. To ensure we knew it was the right car, Charlie would race the engine twice before topping the bridge. When his headlights spotlighted us, Neil and I were in a huge struggle. The whole car erupted into screams as they continued down the road. By then Neil had drug me by the feet to the edge of the creek where we mounted the motor scooter again and sped off toward town with our lights off.

A big dog that loved to chase cars lived at an old farmhouse just outside of town. When we passed there with no lights, the dog heard us, but could no more see us than we could see him. We hit the dog and landed in the ditch by the road with the scooter on top of us. Somehow we managed to get the scooter and ourselves out of the ditch, but we were a real mess. We barely beat Charlie back to the cafe.

When the carload of kids entered the cafe, they were as white as ghosts. One of the girls was pregnant and she was crying about the possible loss of her baby. Everyone talked at once, and most of the stories described a huge monster that had killed a man on the river road. A local policeman came into the cafe and started asking questions of the girls, many of whom seemed to be in shock. Charlie walked over to Neil and me and whispered, "What in the hell happened to you guys?" Apparently none of the others had noticed our cuts and burns from the scooter wreck.

When the local policeman heard several accounts of the monster story, he did just what we hoped he would do—he called for help. A few minutes later, two Oklahoma Highway Patrol units and one County Sheriff drove up. The patrolman asked Charlie to lead the way to the exact location of the alleged attack, so we asked the local policeman if we could ride along with him. He agreed, but told us we would have to remain in the police car once we reached the bridge.

As we approached the bridge, Charlie began to point frantically at the spot. The police units stopped and got out of their cars. They thoroughly searched the area, finding no body or clues, so they concluded that the incident had been a product of the kids' imaginations.

The next day the whole town was talking about the sighting and some people had begun to arm themselves. One of my good friends, who lived only a mile from the site, was not in on the hoax and he stayed up all night sitting at his window with a shotgun. At this point we let the story rest for a couple of weeks, and then as planned, we prepared to use our complete monster wardrobe for another appearance.

For our next adventure, I climbed onto Neil's shoulders with a long coat over us and a pillow on my back to look like a hunchback. Together our distorted body with its scarred face stood over seven-feet tall. We went out to the coal pits where all the lovers parked on weekends. We crept up to the cars making terrible noises while kicking and hitting their vehicles. When utter chaos erupted, we disappeared into a waiting car and headed to the local cafe. Cars poured in from every direction, and the dust from the gravel parking lot blew everywhere. All the people from the coal pits had the same story. A huge monster had attacked them at the coal pits outside of town. The local police arrived on the scene and decided to lead the way to the sighting location. Some people stopped at their homes to get knives and guns.

When we arrived at the coal pits, everyone got out of their cars and looked for clues. Someone found footprints that went straight up a steep coal pit mound. At the base of the mound was a barbed wire fence, so we carefully crawled through the fence and followed the policeman up the steep embankment. Just before the group of over twenty people went over the mound, I screamed, "THERE HE IS!" Everyone turned and scrambled down the embankment, crashing into the barbed wire fence. With all the guns and knives, I don't know how someone did not get hurt. When we got back to the cafe, almost everyone said they had seen the monster! We had successfully created a monster in people's minds.

One day soon after, a businessman from our town made a hysterical report to local police. He said the night before, as he traveled down Old Bird Creek Road, he spotted the monster through his rear view mirror. He claimed that he was traveling over sixty miles per hour and the monster was almost touching his bumper! Our small town hired some extra police to patrol the city, and the County Sherriff's Department also hired some extra men. We knew we had finally made it big when our story reached the Tulsa paper. Some articles compared our story to those of Big Foot and outer space visitors. It was extremely gratifying to Neil, Charlie, and me to have our monster talked about in the same newspaper as legends such as these.

While the monster story seemed to have taken on a life of its own, we decided to plan one final scare. Then it would be time for school to start. Our biggest concern was guns. Many people were carrying them and we did not want to get shot. Our last sighting would be on a lonely country road with a steep hill about two hunded yards above it. Some rocks and bushes on the top of the hill gave us a good place to hide from people and their weapons. On the other side was a prairie with miles and miles of open field and no cross fences. Neil and I would have plenty of room to escape on Gary's motor scooter.

The plan was for Charlie to tell a few people he had spotted the monster on the top of the rocky hill and to bring them up there with no guns. Charlie had a spotlight on top of his car that would reach up to the rocky top. Neil and I in our monster suit would stand up with raised arms and scream a terrifying cry and then duck down the hill and disappear forever. It was a great plan.

As Neil and I waited on the hill for Charlie and the townspeople to arrive, we admired our view. We could see for a couple of miles from our vantage point, and we sat up there looking for car lights heading our direction. To our surprise we soon saw not two or four headlights coming our way, but hundreds! Charlie had apparently told everyone in town he had spotted the monster on the hill. Cars stretched bumper to bumper along the deserted dirt road for what looked like a mile. Charlie began searching the area with his spotlight. I turned to Neil and asked if it was time to stand up. Neil looked at me and said, "You only live once!" We stood up, all seven feet of us, and let out the most blood curdling scream you have ever heard. Charlie's spotlight hit us just like Broadway. The roar from the crowd was followed by gunshots. Neil and I dropped to the ground and crawled on our bellies to our scooter and out of the monster business forever.

To this day, forty years later, this is the first time anyone has ever told the true story of the famous Owasso monster of the 1950's. There are still people who will dispute you if you tell them it was a hoax. Many people in Owasso still believe.

Our house after the remodel and the yard "like a park"
1955

Billboard advertising our parents' first subdivision
1954

Dad, Tom, Sharon, and Gary at Fort Gibson Lake with our new motor boat and 1956 Dodge Convertible

Sharon, Tom, and Gary while visiting the Fullbrights in Arkansas 1951

PART THREE

High School

13

Teacher's Pet

I knew when I started high school that all the boys were expected to take shop while all the girls generally enrolled in glee club. This was not mandatory, but just the way things were in the fifties. I wasn't really interested in shop and on my first day of high school I found out why. When I entered the shop classroom, boys were throwing wood chips at each other and no teacher was in sight. I learned that the shop teacher was in a meeting, so I wandered around the room looking for something to do. I soon discovered the wood lathe to be very intriguing. I mounted a long piece of wood into the lathe and spun it around in the machine at a high speed, thinking I could make a baseball bat. When the teacher entered the room, he ran straight over to my station. He shoved me away from the spinning lathe and leaned over to shut down the machine. His tie got caught in the lathe and almost choked him to death before we got the machine turned off. I was asked to take a different subject.

My only other option was glee club, the all-girl class, but much to my surprise, I loved it. Not only did I have girls to talk to, but the glee club went on overnight road trips, and it turned out to be great fun. Every winter the glee club traveled by bus to Oklahoma State University for a state-wide glee club performance. With every glee club in Oklahoma represented, about six-thousand kids were stretching their vocal chords in the field house at one time. It was fun and exciting to watch the director working to keep us all together.

The weather was cold and during our breaks we could hear the school buses outside running their engines to keep warm while they waited for us to finish our songs. During the last song of the day, I looked up and saw a girl pass out in the upper deck. I kept my eyes on that area and noticed one girl after another collapsing. Kids began to scream and pandemonium spread throughout the field house. At first the director tried to maintain control and keep the music going, but when students began stampeding toward the exits, he stopped the music. More and more kids were passing out and others were throwing up. Someone finally figured out that the carbon monoxide from the buses outside had been sucked into the arena by the air intakes for the heating system. The bus drivers were ordered to turn off their engines and many students were carried out of the building and laid on the ground. Others got very sick and frightened, but fortunately no one died, nor was anyone seriously injured.

I was also taking a speech class my first year, and though my speech teacher was a wonderful person, she was very strict on discipline. She was also very religious. In the fifties, schools were allowed to have religious programs and God could be discussed in the classrooms. I was failing my speech class. My teacher told me that I would get an A in her class if I would sing an acappella solo in the annual Easter program. The song she wanted me to sing was "Were You There." I couldn't refuse the offer because I needed the grade so badly, but I was a terrible singer. So my glee club teacher and my mother worked with me every day for the following weeks leading up to the Easter program, and I actually was beginning to sound pretty good.

The day of the program all the thugs were on the front row in the auditorium ready to laugh me off the stage. Before I made my entrance, a dozen male teachers and a few of the football coaches stood in front of the stage with paddles in their hands to control the crowd. The principal made an announcement saying that anyone who laughed or made noise would be paddled. When I was introduced the audience was perfectly still. I walked out to the center of the stage and sang my song acappella. When I finished, not one person applauded. No one ever told me if it was good or bad. It was as if it had never happened. I did get an A in the class.

My friend Bob and I both failed our English class that first year in high school. In the past I had been able to bribe teachers with favors to get passing grades. It was a big surprise to have a teacher who would rather teach me English than have her house painted or yard work done. We were required to pass English in order to graduate, but Owasso didn't offer summer school, so Bob and I enrolled in an English class at Tulsa Central

High School. On our first day of summer school, I drove Mother's station wagon to Tulsa. On the way there, we passed a large corn field and and we stopped to pick out a few ears for ourselves. Before we knew it, we had filled the whole '54 Ford station wagon. Tulsa Central High was a huge school by our standards; it covered a city block and was three stories high. They graduated close to a thousand students a year compared to Owasso's fifteen or twenty annual graduates. The only parking spot that remained in the lot was right in front of classroom windows, and our car was full of corn. Kids noticed the two country boys outside and pointed and laughed at us. I decided to play the role and stood by the car nibbling on an ear of corn. The teacher looked out the window and ordered me to get to my classroom.

She had not noticed Bob, but he didn't like her telling me what to do, so he grabbed a large ear of corn and threw it toward the window. It was a great shot and went in the window in which the teacher had appeared just moments before. The teacher jumped to the window and looked down at me and yelled, "Don't move!" A few minutes went by and I stood on the curb waiting to see what would happen. Then the teacher appeared with the corn and the principal of the school. I was taken to the office and questioned, but in my section of the world, a kid died before telling on a friend, so I remained in trouble.

The principal told me to leave school at once or he would call the police. "What can I do to make up for what happened?" I asked him, explaining that I had to have a passing grade.

"Nothing," he said. "Get out right now." As I was being escorted out of the office, Bob walked up and gently said, "Sir, you have the wrong man. I threw the corn." I was so relieved, but not for long.

"I don't care. You both are out of here," the principal said.

The next day my parents went with me and persuaded the principal to give Bob and me another chance to make our grade.

14

Sixteen at Last

When I turned sixteen, my life started to change quickly. The wild geese flying south for the winter and the leaves falling off the trees took on a different meaning. When you grow up in the country, you are more aware of the seasonal changes in nature. The passing of the years were more significant. I felt a new sense of urgency to live every day to its fullest and work as hard as possible to find new adventures. This change came about because I was old enough to understand the gravity of my doctor's dire prediction that I wouldn't live to be more than thirty years old. That meant I only had fourteen years left.

Since I was now of legal age to drive a car, I asked the school principal if I could take off to get my driver's license. Only a few kids at my school had cars, so many of the sixteen-year-olds without cars wanted to go with me and use my parents' car to take their driving test. That same day we had a school assembly, and the principal announced to the student body that six young men from our school were headed to Collinsville to take their driver's tests. He warned everyone to stay off the highway.

On the way to Collinsville, I was amazed to learn that the other five boys had read and studied for the test. I laughed at them and made jokes about how hard the test could possibly be. After all, I had been driving around our farm for over two years. When I got inside and was handed my copy of the test, I couldn't believe how stupid the questions were—like, "How close should you park to the curb?"

"As close as you can get," I wrote. Apparently they wanted more specific answers, so I failed the written test. The next time I read and studied all the materials and made a perfect score. Since I was an accomplished driver, I thought the driving part of the test would be a snap. Well, I ran five stop signs and failed. I was eighteen before I finally passed.

Gary also drove for several years before he had a license, but he was more inclined to take chances driving out on the main highway, particularly when one of our parents' vehicles was readily available. One afternoon my parents were having new carpet installed in our house and they asked me to stay home to meet the carpet layers. Ronnie came over and we were sitting on the front porch waiting for them to finish the job. We noticed Dad's car coming up the road at full speed, but as it turned into the drive, we saw Gary at the wheel. He jumped out of the car and ran into the house as fast as he could. "The police are after me!" he yelled.

A few minutes later an Oklahoma Highway Patrolman drove into our driveway. He asked Ronnie and me if the driver of our car was in the house. We told the officer we hadn't seen him, but to our surprise he already knew Gary's full name and address. "I'll wait out here until he comes out," the patrolman said, so we figured we'd better go inside and find Gary. He was hiding in the closet. He told us he was stopped for speeding and that he had told the policeman his driver's license was at home. The patrolman told Gary to go on home and he would radio a dispatcher to make sure he had a valid Oklahoma driver's license. If he did not, he would come to his house and take him to jail. Gary was scared to death. With the police on our front porch and Mother and Dad due home at any time, he was trapped.

The carpet layers were just finishing up and began to roll up the old carpet they had removed. While they were loading one roll into the van, Ronnie and I quickly rolled Gary up into the largest piece. The carpet layers unknowingly picked it up with Gary inside and carried it right by the policeman and loaded it into the van. As they drove off, my parents came into the driveway. Together with the policeman, they searched the entire house and the grounds. Finally, the policeman gave up and left.

When the carpet layers reached town, Gary started hollering from the back of the van. They stopped, ran to the back of their truck, and unrolled the fugitive. Gary took off and ran to a girl's house and hid out the rest of the day. Later that night the girl's parents called and told my parents to come and get their son. Mother and Dad went into town and had the policeman meet them there. He gave Gary a good scare and a steep ticket, but let him go home.

I, too, took some chances. Gary was a great basketball player in high school and was dating a very attractive girl during basketball season. One day I overheard them talking about going somewhere to park after the game. I heard his girlfriend say that Gary "would get what he had been wanting." Gary was so excited he could hardly dribble the basketball that night. He had asked Mother if he could drive her new Ford station wagon and she had agreed, warning him to be careful. So during the game, ten of my friends and I found the car keys under the seat of the wagon parked in the parking lot. We loaded up to take a spin in the country. The car had a standard transmission and was far overloaded. We were approximately two miles from town when I popped the clutch and blew out the transmission. We all got out and pushed the car back to town, rolling it back into its exact tracks just in time to catch the end of the game.

Gary's team won and his girlfriend was all over him. After he showered they went out and got in the station wagon and Gary put the car into gear. Nothing happened. Gary jumped out of the car screaming mad and chased me all over the gym. Not only did he get blamed for the transmission, his date left with another player.

Driving around in cars was a big thrill in high school. Between the time when I failed my first drivers' test and the age of eighteen when I finally got licensed, I learned how to drive with my feet and break all the local speed records in Owasso. The guy with the fastest, coolest car got the best girls and the most attention from everyone. It was cool to live dangerously, but I'm not sure how my friends and I made it through high school alive. In a small town, which Owasso definitely was, a boy had to prove himself in any number of ways. One of these tests was a successful run over the Bird Creek Bridge.

My friend Jack held the driving record on Bird Creek Bridge. His top speed was seventy-five miles per hour. The hardest part about obtaining a record of this nature was finding a person brave enough to ride in the back of the car to witness the speed. Also the bridge was dangerous for three reasons. First of all, it was a one lane bridge. Second, the bridge had wood runners on the top because it was built before concrete bridges. The third reason was the most important—the bridge had an up ramp and a down ramp followed by a hair pin curve at the end of the bridge. I knew with all these factors to consider, it would be a tough go to break Jack's Bird Creek record.

With two extremely dumb people for witnesses in the back of my dad's car, and an ignorant person driving, I set the car on ninety miles per hour. I don't think we ever hit the bottom of the bridge all the way across, and of course we did not make the curve. Soon Dad's car, the witnesses, and I were in the pecan orchard next to the bridge. Much to our surprise and relief, the car wasn't damaged and our bodies were intact.

For the next few years following my Bird Creek run, I was notorious for all kinds of car stunts. Every Friday night all the small town kids drove to Tulsa.

Admiral Boulevard was a four lane street with a traffic light every mile. This street was the track for nightly drag racing. We left Owasso and raced to Tulsa and did the drag scene on Admiral all night. When it was time to go home, we raced like hell down a narrow road with no shoulders all the way back. Every curve and bridge was a death trap for teenage dragsters.

The new highway was under construction at this time, and at night the state highway department lowered the arm of a huge crane across the road. This arm kept people off the new highway at night. Everyone, except my crazy friend Bob, accepted this restriction, but Bob would do anything for a laugh. Bob's dad had a new Cadillac. He was proud of the fact his car cost more than his whole farm. One Friday night Bob and I took the new car down the new highway. When we came to the crane with the arm extending across the road, we noticed it was just high enough by a few inches to go underneath. In the clear, we took off for Tulsa and Cotton's Drive Inn.

When we arrived we bet everyone in the place we could beat anyone driving back to Owasso. So later that night as people rallied to leave, we once again extended our challenge. The race began from Cotton's and Bob and I pulled out into the lead. With everyone catching up, we pulled off the old highway onto the new unfinished highway. Everyone in the race shot by us honking and laughing. They all knew we would get trapped by the crane and not get through. But Bob and I figured we would beat them all and be sitting on the hood of the car on Main Street by the time they turned the last corner into town.

We were cruising along at about a hundred miles per hour when we saw the crane up ahead in the road. We were too busy laughing about how stupid everyone else was to notice something was about to go wrong. For some reason we had made it under the crane arm safely at the slow speed, but when we hit the crane going this fast, something had changed. We tore the top off of the new Caddy and never made it to Main Street.

Thinking back on those times, I realize we did whatever it took to get as close to the edge of death in a car as we could. I still don't know how we lived through those days. Not only should I have been dead, we could have easily killed many others. Our new friend Benny owned a 1958 Corvette. Every boys' dream was to own a car, especially a Corvette! One weekend we took Benny's Corvette to the lake, passing thirty or forty cars at a time moving along at about a hundred miles per hour. Passing all those cars that fast was dangerous enough, but we also had about six guys piled in a car built for two. At one point on the trip, I was lying on the back of the car and my feet touched the concrete. The heat got my attention fast because I burned the ends of my shoes off in just a few seconds.

After football games everyone got in cars and raced from Owasso to Tulsa. We raced trucks, cars, motor bikes, and any other road vehicle all the way there and then later raced home. All of us tried to win. One night I was riding in the back of a pickup truck and Jack was in his parents' '57 Chevy. He tried to pass us on the narrow two lane road. As he came up beside us, I grabbed a ten foot log chain lying in the back of the pickup. I swung it around and around like a lasso, and when Jack pulled up close, I hit him across the head lamps and grill. This made him slam on the brakes and we pulled out ahead. Jack decided to try one more pass. This time, when I threw the log chain, it knocked out a head lamp and the chain hooked on the bumper. Jack hit his brakes again, but this time I was holding on to the chain and got pulled right out of the pickup. I landed face-down on the concrete, smashing my nose and face and burning the skin off my hands. Then Jack almost ran over me. I looked pretty bad for a few weeks.

Another night at Cotton's Drive Inn, I was in my parents' '54 Ford station wagon and I must have had six or eight riders with me. When we reached the traffic circle at the city limits of Tulsa, a highway patrolman watched me go around the circle. Just out of stupidity I guess, I did not turn off to go home; I just kept going around and around and around until nearly everyone in the car was green, begging me to stop. Finally the patrolman stopped me and wrote out a citation. "What's this ticket for, officer?" I asked.

"You haven't broken any laws," he said. "You just deserve one."

One afternoon I was cruising down the highway heading to Tulsa and I noticed a bread truck preparing to cross the intersection. As I approached the crossing, he pulled out in front of me and I broadsided him. The bread truck spun around in circles and covered the highway with bread and cupcakes. No one was hurt, but it totaled my parents' car. I got three tickets and my drivers' license was suspended for six months. This may be one of the reasons I didn't get killed. I knew I had to be very careful from then on.

15

Football

Every Friday night in the fall was football night in Owasso. Most people in small towns, especially in Oklahoma, love sports. The football game was the event of the week. and nearly everyone in town turned out for the game. As popular as football was for the locals, it was even a bigger deal for the kids at school. No matter if you were big or small, weak or strong, untalented or agile, every boy wanted to play on the football team. Without football you were a nobody.

I had the same choice as any other kid at my school. I could try out for the football team and hope to be a town hero, or I could sit around on the bleachers with the other losers from school. Most of my friends decided to hang out on the bleachers, but I went for the gold. I qualified for the team and began to practice for hours at a time. As I worked hard running lap after lap around the track, I watched my friends with all the girls. I'm not sure if I made the right decision, but football became my life.

One thing that was hard to get used to was the locker room. All the players walked around naked and acted like it was normal. When a kid sees everyone naked for the first time, he realizes how different and interesting each person can be. One kid named Buck was covered with hair and looked like an ape. Every boy was a different shape and size.

The other thing I had to get used to was the horrible smell of a locker room. Some of the players actually took pride in not washing their clothes—even their jock straps. My biggest fear was getting jock itch. One of my teammates got jock itch so bad he had to keep the top button of his shirt buttoned because of his rash. He was one of the guys who never showered or washed his jock strap.

Our football coach believed a kid had to be tough to play ball. If someone got hurt during practice, the coach left him lying there and ran plays all over his body. We were not allowed to leave the field to get a drink during practice. If a player did get hurt or needed a drink, Coach called him a "cull." The name cull was his favorite for anyone who did not measure up to his expectations. We suffered out there for hours because we were afraid of him. It's a wonder that someone didn't die from being forced to run and play football with no water to drink for two or three hours in the hot sun. If a coach did that today, he'd be fired, but in the fifties it was common practice.

Our coach's name was Bull, and projecting a tough image was very important to him. Consequently we questioned his choice of a car. He drove a Henry J and he loved his little car and kept it in great shape, but it was a cull. The only thing tough about it was that Bull would kill you if you touched it.

Bull usually ran to and from the practice field with the team after school every day, but one afternoon a teammate and I had gotten into some kind of trouble with Bull and he made us stay in the locker room and clean it out for punishment. Then he surprised us by asking me if I would drive his car over to the field when we got through. He was going to have to leave practice early for an appointment so he wanted his car to be there. I agreed and assured him I would be careful. It occurred to my friend and me that if we didn't clean the locker room we would have time to make a quick run into Tulsa in the Henry J. So we got in the car and fired up the engine when Bull and the other players were out of sight. It was a lot of fun driving that little car around Cotton's Drive Inn in our big padded uniforms. We thought we could get back in time for football practice, but it was nearly over by the time we returned. Bull was hot. Taking his car was a big mistake. He made us run thousands of laps over the next few years, and he also called me the "King of the Culls" the rest of my high school career.

One kid on our team was called "Double Tough." He was the biggest kid in school and weighed around three hundred pounds. He was not only big, but mean too, and Bull loved to play him. The only problem was his vision. Double Tough was nearly blind, so in order to play football, he had to wear glasses as thick as coke bottles.

We didn't have face masks on our helmets in those days, so when Double Tough practiced, he taped his glasses on and told everyone not to hit him in the face.

None of us would have been that crazy, but it was nice that he gave us a warning. In our first game of the year, Double Tough taped on his glasses and went on to the field, but the referees wouldn't let him play with his glasses on. He had to sit on the bench and without him we got far behind. The local fans got nervous and started chanting, "Put in Double Tough, Put in Double Tough."

Apparently Bull couldn't stand the pressure because he grabbed Double Tough for a play and sent him in with no glasses. The crowd went nuts! Bull should have realized he made a mistake when Double Tough had trouble finding the huddle, but our quarterback handed off the ball to Double Tough, and he went straight up the middle. He was fast, considering how big he was, and he gained yards on the play by hitting the line and knocking tacklers in every direction. The tragedy happened when he was hit and spun around and then ran straight for his own goal line! Our whole team chased after him in hopes of bringing him down, but Double Tough made a great eighty yard run in the wrong direction. Then the fans yelled, "Take out Double Tough, Take out Double Tough."

The telltale sign of a fifties football player was a broken nose and missing teeth. Without face masks the whole game was different. By 1957 the face mask became standard equipment and the frame of it was made out of two-inch wide Plexiglas. The players loved them for protection, but even more so for tackling. At that time it wasn't illegal to grab onto a face mask to bring someone down when making a tackle. That is no longer true, for good reason. If you grabbed a face mask, an opponent followed anywhere.

One night I was ready for the Friday night game and I went into the dressing room a little early. When I got there, I saw one of our running backs, Charlie, sharpening the frame of his face mask with a file. By the time he got finished, it was razor sharp. He told me he was tired of getting tackled by his face mask. I told Charlie that someone could get their fingers cut off if they grabbed his mask, but Charlie just looked at me and said, "That's good."

In the huddle just as the game began, Charlie told me to watch for the first player that grabbed his mask. Charlie's number was called, and when he got the ball he headed through the line. A kid on the other team ran up to Charlie but didn't grab his mask. Instead he tackled Charlie with his arm stretched out underneath Charlie's mask, forcing his mask off. His face mask caught Charlie in the forehead and literally scalped him. He left the field screaming. When he stood in front of Bull with his scalp laying open and blood dripping down his face, Bull shook his head and said, "What a cull." After a few hundred stitches, Charlie was okay, but he was forbidden to play in the next few games and was prematurely bald.

One of my teammates, Wes, had a heart condition. He played half back and used to pass out when the team was not doing well. Whenever the team started doing better, he was always ready to go back in. Once Wes blacked out just before half-time. He was carried off the field so a doctor could look at him during the half-time festivities. For some reason that night, they blacked out the stadium for the band's performance. When Wes woke up in the darkness, he made a fool of himself by running around the field yelling, "I've gone blind!"

Before each game, the team gathered in the locker room to get ready to run through a paper covered hoop on the way out onto the field. The night I got to lead the team out, I tripped on the ring and fell to the ground. The whole team, including the coaches, ran over my back and all I remember is someone calling me a cull as they trampled my body.

The truth was that we were all culls. I doubt if any of us could have had dates the way we acted, but it didn't matter because Bull didn't allow anyone to date the night before the game. In fact, if he could have had total control, he would have forbidden dating altogether. He believed if we got hot and bothered, we wouldn't stay in shape or keep our minds on football.

I don't think that's what our problem was. What our team really needed was a leader. We needed a quarterback to pull the team together and throw the football. One summer a new kid moved into town. My friends and I drove by his house to check him out. He was out in the street throwing a ball to a kid that was almost a block away! I'd never seen anyone with this kind of ability. We decided to make friends with this new kid and ease him in to our way of thinking. We learned his name was Jim and we asked him to go for a ride with us. We tested his courage by taking him for a death ride—driving down the highway at breakneck speeds. Then we had a spit fight. This was a good test because it was almost too gross for the regular bunch, much less a new friend. Jim passed all our tests.

The interesting thing about Jim was his forehead. It stuck out two or three inches beyond his eyes, and it made him look like a caveman. His skull was also large and hard. I found this out a few years later when we came out of a nightclub in Tulsa and a man hit Jim as hard as he could with a solid oak ax handle. Jim started bleeding, but he calmly stood there and said, "What the hell did you do that for?" The man who hit him apologized by saying he had been waiting on someone else and had hit the wrong guy. Jim said it was okay and he went to the hospital for a few stitches.

Jim never did get to play football for Owasso High School. I thought he would be perfect for our team, but when he went out for football, they couldn't find a helmet to fit him. Jim also liked to drink and smoke, and he would never have kept the no dating rule, but he became one of our good friends.

16

Mom Hits the Road

I had just begun my junior year of high school and I was looking forward to my next two years. I had not been around the house much to know what was going on with my mother. I came home after school one day to find her packing her bag. I had seen her do this before, but she never got much further than the front door before she'd be back. This time she looked different. She was dressed in preppy clothes and looked like a college girl. She even had on a pair of sneakers, and those shoes made me suspicious. Mom had always wanted to be a medical doctor. She got married young, started a family early, and eventually she gave up on her dream, but she never forgot about it. When Dad got home that evening, Mom gathered the family in the den and told us good-bye. She left the very next day to go to Oklahoma State University in Stillwater to enroll as a freshman in college. She moved into the women's dorm and never looked back. Eleven years later we all celebrated her return to Owasso. With her she brought a license to practice medicine.

My mother's initial departure changed the lives of everyone in our family. It left my dad and me alone in the house for my last two years of high school. My sister Sharon was getting ready for college too, but decided to run off and marry a wonderful man named Ed Collins, who later became like a brother to me. They remain married today. My brother Gary also got married and is still married, but not to the same person. What little structure we had in our household had been due to my mother. Though her leaving did give me the opportunity to live my last two years at home with no supervision, it was not what I needed. No one was there to cook. I did what cleaning there was to do, and Dad paid the bills. I had complete freedom and thought I didn't care.

Mom leaving to go to school meant that Dad had total control over their real estate business. By that time they had built some of their own apartment buildings. One complex had twenty units, and while Mother was away at school, Dad managed to fill all twenty rooms with women. When Mom came home for a visit, she had a house cleaning. Not just the dirt went, but so did all the women who were not paying rent. She then insisted that Dad hire an apartment manager.

Dad also had bought an old building that at one time had been a movie theater in Owasso. For a short while, Gary even worked there until he accidentally left the projector light on too long and somehow caught the film on fire. The whole theater had to be evacuated. Dad decided to convert the old building into rental offices after my Mom left. He and I went inside to clean the place up and, like all movie theaters, the floor ran downhill. There had apparently been a water leak somewhere because the area just below the screen had filled with water. Following a hard rain, the water would get waist deep, so Dad and I installed a sump pump in the lowest corner.

One particular rainy afternoon, Dad noticed something stuck in the pump blocking the flow of water. He took off his shoes and pants, waded into the water, and without realizing it, he grabbed a hot wire that was protruding from the pump. A tremendous bolt of electricity shook his body to the roots and I thought he was going to be cremated. I really got a laugh though after I realized he was okay.

17

Dangerous Encounters

As I look back over the years, I think my friends and I were on a one-way street to self-destruction. I don't know if it was our upbringing, the era we grew up in, or a combination of both. We had no meaning in our lives, no direction, and no heroes. I remember many times when it seemed like we were trying to kill ourselves. We played games like running as fast as we could and then jumping to see who could land closest to the edge of a one-hundred-foot bluff without going over. In the fifties we lived in fear of communism, hordes of Chinese, tornadoes, floods, polio, atomic bombs, and the Lord due to arrive any day. We had drills every month at school to practice what we should do in the event of an atomic bomb attack. These things weighed heavily on our minds.

One night walking home, I looked up in the sky and saw thousands of airplanes heading toward Tulsa. I figured this was the end of it all and I ran home to warn anyone I saw of the impending disaster. I fully expected to see a brilliant flash of light signaling the end of my life as I knew it. What I had seen were stars within a thin, fast-moving cloud cover making it appear that the stars were moving or thousands of airplanes were swarming to drop bombs. With fear like this, it didn't make any sense to worry about the future. I lost several friends from automobile accidents and three more from suicides. I always thought I would be the one killed, not my friends.

Some of my classmates quit school in the tenth grade. Some got married, others joined the military, and a few in town actually got jobs. One of my good friends joined the Marine Corps. He had only been gone for a few weeks before I noticed one day he was back. I asked him about his return and told him I thought boot camp lasted for three or four months. He told me that shortly after he arrived there, he got a medical discharge. I couldn't believe it and so I asked to see his papers. The reason for his discharge was that he was too immature! I think any of my friends would have received the same discharge if we had joined at this time in our life.

Everything we did had a sense of urgency to it, as if we expected no tomorrow. I can remember very well thinking it wasn't important to get my school work done, because I believed I might not be alive the following day. That line of thinking is probably the reason my friends and I played so hard and dangerously.

One of our favorite dangerous games to play was chicken with freight trains. We stood on the tracks and tried to see who could wait the longest in front of the train without getting run over. When this became boring we threw rocks at the boxcars as they went by at high speeds. One day when I was particularly bored, I picked up a large rock and threw it at an oncoming boxcar. When it hit the end of the car, it was as if it had been struck by a baseball bat; the rock came straight back at me. I ducked just in time, but as the rock flew over my head I heard one of my friends yell. The rock had hit him in the face and he was lying still on the ground. I thought I had killed him. We all gathered around and made a pact not to tell anyone what had happened to our friend. We covered his body with gravel and dirt, and then threw grass and brush on top. We formulated a story to tell his parents, but what could we say without getting in big trouble?

As we were walking away, we heard a noise and turned to see our friend sitting up, asking what had happened to him! We were so glad to see him alive we carried him home on our shoulders. He asked several times why he was covered up with dirt and rocks. Lucky for me, my friends and I never told what had really happened. This incident may seem serious, but it was just one among many dangerous encounters I had.

It started out as an innocent trip to the dump to dispose of some trash for Jack's family—a typical experience for Jack and me. The dump on their farm was a washed-out area that was filled with trash and then later covered with dirt on top of the trash for fill. The dirt hid the waste and prevented erosion. Jack hooked up a two-wheel trailer to his hitch on the pickup truck, and off we went. Not long after we dumped the trash, I noticed something was wrong with our setup. The trailer was not snugly resting on the hitch and Jack was driving only about ten miles per hour. In order to provide weight and stabilize the two-wheel trailer, I got out of the truck and stood up on the trailer over the axle. When I inadvertently stepped back toward the rear of the trailer, it completely came loose from the hitch and continued to roll on its own just as Jack looked in his rearview mirror at me. He laughed.

The trailer and I slowly rolled to a stop, and Jack jumped out of the truck and came running back to me. "Hey! I want to try that!" he said. I drove the truck and pulled Jack up to twenty miles per hour, and he then stepped back to release the trailer which carried him across the open prairie. Riding the trailer was lots of fun—so much fun that we drove into town and picked up some friends to take on our new ride.

We approached such speeds as forty, fifty, and sixty miles per hour across the pasture, yelling all the time about riding a free wheel. One time Ronnie and I rode double. We sat side by side on the trailer, and when Jack waved his arm it meant we were riding close to seventy miles per hour. At that point we leaned back and the trailer rose off the hitch, sending us on a wild ride. For some reason we both sat back up at the same time, and when we did, the trailer tongue dropped down and hit the dirt, throwing us off the trailer as if we were on one of those medieval catapults. We laughed hysterically. It was time to up the ante.

We couldn't get the truck up over seventy miles per hour on the prairie, so we took our rig to the highway. I don't know how fast we were going when Jack waved his hand, but we shot off the truck between two large trees, went through a barbed wire fence, and the trailer landed upside down in a garden. We left it there and never went back.

A rancher named Ralph frequented the pool hall. He owned a debt-free ten-thousand-acre ranch that was one of the most beautiful ranches in Oklahoma. It had a large country style home on it and thousands of registered Hereford cattle grazed on the blue stem grass. Ralph was only twenty-three years old and dressed in the finest cowboy wear.

Sometimes Ralph called me to drive him in his Cadillac to the sale barn in Collinsville so he could drink and stay out of trouble. At least twice on these trips to town, he became angry over something and threw his bottle out of the window, breaking the glass because he didn't realize the window was up. Later on Ralph bought a four-seat airplane, but he didn't know how to fly. My friend Jack took lessons and got his pilots' license so he could fly Ralph all around the state. When Ralph grew tired of flying, he told Jack to fly whenever he wanted to and sign for all the gas. This was a great benefit for Jack and me because we had our own plane and all the fuel we needed.

Often we took off from Riverside Airport and landed the plane on Jack's farm. Uncle Cys, Jack's dad, was usually there shaking his head and muttering to himself about us being dumb sons-of-bitches. Our usual strategy on those days was to take off the doors of the plane and load it up with as many rocks as it could carry. Then we took off and flew around looking for dairy barns to bomb. Our favorite target was the McClue Dairy. Not only was the barn large, but Jerry McClue went to school with us. We loved the idea of him going out to clean up the messes we made at his farm. We flew over low and threw out the rocks to land on top of his metal barn. When the rocks hit, cows ran out of the barn, and some still had milking machines strapped to them.

One afternoon Jack, Ronnie, and I went out flying, and Jack told us about a new trick he learned in flying school. He told us to hold on and the next thing we knew he went for an outside loop. The g-force was so great I felt my face stretched back and, when I looked in the back seat, Ronnie's face looked like he was in a cyclotron machine. I didn't worry much until I forced my head over to look at Jack, and he looked the same but his hands were not on the stick. Then I heard rivets come loose in the wings of the plane, and I knew we'd had it. However, this time I was wrong. The plane somehow straightened itself out, and we made it back to the airport with enough ignorance leftover to try it again another day.

Ronnie and I flew one more time with Jack. This time we landed in the pasture behind my house and we couldn't get enough speed to take off again without running into a fence. To attempt the take-off, we unloaded Ronnie and all the gear we didn't need. Then we began to move and gain speed, and at the last second before we hit the fence, Jack pulled back hard on the stick and we cleared the fence and were on our way.

We never flew again. About six years after Ralph bought the plane, he died of liver problems. He was lonely and broke, and I had watched him go from what I thought was the very top of the world to a broken and sad ending. At the time he died, the plane was worth thirty thousand dollars, but it sold for a seventy-five hundred dollar fuel bill.

18

Senior Year

By the time I became a senior in high school, I thought I had all the answers. The world had better watch out because I was coming through. What a joke that was! I had no idea of what lay ahead. All that mattered was that I was going to have fun. In the back of my mind I expected to have just thirteen years left to live, and I wanted to live every day of my life to the fullest.

Even though I was wild and spontaneous my senior year, I was proud of myself for making sure other kids in my class had fun too. I had been belittled and teased when I was younger, so I knew how it felt and that made me sensitive to kids who didn't fit in. I danced with the wallflowers at school dances and encouraged my friends to do the same. Years later classmates told me they appreciated my kindness; others probably thought I was a jerk.

My class had changed a great deal over our last year in high school. Many of my friends had quit school to join the military, and others had married and started families. I couldn't believe that anyone at the age of fourteen, fifteen, or sixteen wanted kids, but some did.

When graduation finally rolled around, I wondered for the first time what I was going to do after high school. Nobody, including my teachers and parents, offered any suggestions to help me figure out my future. I concluded that I could either go into business with my dad, or try for a college athletic scholarship. Until that decision had to be made, I was committed to full-time enjoyment of the last few weeks of being a senior.

Each graduating class before us had gone on an overnight senior trip just before the last week of school. The class just before us had gone completely crazy and caused a lot of trouble on their senior trip, so a new policy was established that prohibited overnight stays. It was a challenge to think of something fun, wild, and memorable to do for our senior trip when we had to be in Owasso for the night. We eventually came up with the idea to go to Oklahoma City to the Spring Lake Amusement Park on Saturday, and then return to Owasso and go to Fort Gibson Lake the next day.

The amusement park was fun, but it was not nearly as interesting as the problems which arose at the lake. Pinball Johnny brought along some of his dad's home brew. Though no one drank more than one glassful, it was enough to make us want to act drunk. A guy named J.D. ran out in front of the whole class in his new speedo, and swung from tree to tree acting like an ape. The teachers and girls all hid their eyes and screamed because his bathing suit was nothing more than a colored jock strap. It was a great "class bonding" kind of moment.

The last day of school I organized a walkout for the seniors. I had planned a walkout before in high school, but it hadn't worked. I was the only one who walked out, and I got fifteen licks with a paddle for it. I was afraid the senior walkout would turn out the same way, but when I rang the bell, about half of the seniors got up in the middle of class and left. It was great. I was really surprised and we had a wonderful day.

Our strict English teacher didn't think the walkout was funny at all. She gave a pop quiz in class on that day, and those of us who left had to make up the test or we would fail. A failing English grade was enough to keep any senior from graduation. Even though I could have made an F on the make-up test and graduated, I refused to take it, so I was the only one in my class who did not graduate.

By then I had decided that I really wanted to play football in college, so I have seriously questioned why I refused to take that test. Mom came home for the summer after school was out and I told both my parents that I was thinking about going to college. "Good luck," was all my dad had to say about it, and I don't remember any response from my mother. They didn't ask me any questions as to where I might want to go or how I might pay for it. Dad had other things on his mind. He had bought a family membership in a country club. "Now we'll all have a place to swim, golf, and play tennis," he boasted.

My family was not part of the country club scene to say the least. We had never played tennis, we didn't own golf clubs, and all our swimming was done in a stock pond. We did, however, have years of experience pretending like we were something we were not. Putting on a front for a group of high society types did not seem to pose a problem. Our first day at the club was a Saturday. When Mom, Dad, and I arrived, I went straight to the pool to swim. I found three diving boards and lots of good-looking girls there. Since I spent a good deal of time walking through cow shit on our farm, my bare feet did not look their best. My toenails were a funky shade of orange. As I stood poolside checking out the scene, a kid walked up in a suit and tie and said, "You didn't brush your toes." I had never heard of such a thing, so I shoved him into the pool. The suit and tie boy turned out to be the manager's son.

While I was making my entrance at the pool, my mother teed off for the first time on the golf course. She had never played golf before. When she got to the green, she saw four golf balls scattered about, thinking they were there for the taking. She got so excited, she picked them up. The four women who were playing those balls ran toward the green screaming obscenities at her, and although Mom apologized, one lady did not stop screaming. Mom hit her in the head with her putter. It didn't help that there were three other women who witnessed her aggressive act.

Meanwhile Dad was checking out the plush clubhouse with its ballroom and fancy eating facility. He was eager to establish himself as a bona fide new member among the office staff. That might have been all right until he was caught making out with the club manager's secretary. Tuesday we received a letter which told us we were out of the club.

I spent that summer working out and training for football. My plan was to try out for one of the athletic scholarships at Northeastern Oklahoma Junior College in Miami, Oklahoma. It was a long shot because of my failing English grade on my high school transcript, the fact that I hadn't actually graduated, and I would still have to take entrance exams. I knew that any chance of succeeding in college would be increased if I could get away from my old friend Bob. An association with Bob meant trouble. He was old baggage, and I wanted a clean start with new friends. I told Bob I was going out for football at Coffeyville Junior College in Kansas. Bob did as I expected and enrolled there.

Football practice in Miami began two weeks before the start of the fall semester in the middle of August. The temperature was one hundred plus degrees and it was very, very sticky. Football camp was called Hell Weeks, and hell they were. I was one of the smallest players at camp weighing 165 pounds and standing five foot eight inches tall. There were about 300 players trying out from all over the United States. Their average size was six feet tall and 230 pounds. All I had going for me was my strength and my endurance. The number dropped to 200 players by the end of the first week, and by the end of the second hell week, we were down to 100. Thirty of those were returning scholarship recipients from the year before. Thirty more athletic scholarships were to be awarded to new players.

After the final practice, 100 guys were gathered out on the courtyard waiting to be called in for a personal meeting with the head coach. There we would learn if we had earned one of the coveted thirty scholarships. One by one our names were called. The longer I waited, the more I agonized and assumed the worst. I was the last man to be called, so it was a huge surprise and delight when the coach offered me both a scholarship and a guaranteed job. I couldn't wait to go home and tell my parents. When I got there and shared my good news, they didn't even know I'd been gone for two weeks.

That hurt, but I was okay. Lucky for me I was never required to take any entrance exam, nor was I asked to produce a high school transcript. I was on my way to college. I hoped that my childish ways were over. I had seen so many people screw up their lives, and some even lose theirs, so the fact that I hadn't spent time in jail or gotten killed or maimed by all the fun and games must have meant I'd done something right. Though I had no real guidelines to live by, I'd had some good friends I trusted and who trusted me. I always thought my friends had more problems than I did, so I tried to help them.

I still never thought I would live to see thirty, and I had never truly contemplated what it meant to be responsible. Yet I cared about my family and I had watched out for them. I tried to protect my brother and sister from any harm and I wouldn't let anyone say anything bad about my family. I may have even acquired some new insight as to why I didn't take that last English test. I didn't realize it at the time, but all I was looking for, and all that I needed, was someone to care.

*Traffic bottleneck on Highway 169 leading to the
single-lane Bird Creek Bridge
1953*

*Sharon, Owasso High School Band Queen, riding in
Owasso Progress Day Parade, Gary driving our new
1958 Chevrolet convertible*

Gary, Sharon, and Tom in our home the night
of Tom's graduation
1960

Owasso High School Rams
Tom # 44, middle row, and Bob # 36, back row
1960

*Tom as guard for the Owasso Rams the year he was
nominated for All-State Team
1960*

Tom Sherrill, Senior year
1960

Made in the USA
Monee, IL
07 July 2026

56552164R00104